The Practical Manager's Guide to Excellence in Management

The Practical Manager's Guide to Excellence in Management

RONALD BROWN

amacom

A DIVISION OF AMERICAN MANAGEMENT ASSOCIATIONS

TO MY WIFE

THIS BOOK WAS SET IN ASTER BY BOOK COMPOSITION SERVICES.
IT WAS DESIGNED BY JOAN GREENFIELD.
PRINTER AND BINDER WAS ALPINE PRESS.

Library of Congress Cataloging in Publication Data

Brown, Ronald, 1900–
    The practical manager's guide to excellence in
management.

    Includes index.
    1. Management.   I. Title.   II. Title: Excellence
in management.
HD31.B7667   658.4   79–11883
ISBN 0–8144–5520–4

© 1979 AMACOM
A division of American Management Associations, New York.
All rights reserved. Printed in the United States of America.

First Printing

Preface

Management in its broadest sense is an exciting, enticing, challenging function. Once achieved, it takes on another aspect. For those in the top managerial echelons, it is often a case of "the higher up, the closer to the door." For the sole owner or principal shareholder, it provides at times a life of tensions, pressures, and fears that dilute the pleasure of the experience. For those below the top management echelons, the work is frequently full of stresses and strains that dilute the effectiveness of the manager.

All this can be avoided. There is no reason why a good manager cannot be continually on top of his job, confident, secure, happy in his work, and extremely effective whatever echelon he occupies. This can be accomplished through some of the ideas described in the following pages.

The purpose of this book is not to provide a "patent medicine" for management ailments. Rather, it is to stimulate thinking about the managerial function so as to create a new environment for operating as a manager, a better understanding of what comprises the job, and a better way of performing the job. It should give the manager the satisfaction of knowing that he has a good team around him, that his results and those of the entire organization are benefiting from the achievements of himself and his team.

When we talk about the people who work "under" the manager, we mean those whom the manager needs to help achieve his objectives. These people must operate within a framework set by the manager, one for which he accepts complete responsibility. They may be men or women, veterans or new employees, highly promotable or marginal. But while they can share in much of the planning and are indispensable in operations, they must accept the manager's final decision-making authority.

Those referred to in the text as subordinates will themselves often be managers. The term "subordinate" means simply that the person is accepting a portion of the manager's job. To the extent that the manager is accountable for the performance of the total job, he must exercise his authority and responsibility.

There is one exception: employees affected by the unionization of an operation. In such cases, both employees and employers are subject to various agreements growing out of union contracts and the decisions of arbitrators, grievance committees, or the equivalent.

The ideas set forth in this book are a product of the author's exposure to the management operations of many corporations, a school board, a library board, a division of a large university, a state commission, and several social agencies, as well as his experience as an executive of an international business organization that he helped to found and served for over 30 years.

The book makes no claim to perfection. It simply represents one manager talking informally to another manager, sharing his experiences. All of us learn from our daily successes and failures, and these pages reflect a written record of the learning experience of one manager.

Ronald Brown

Contents

1

What Is Management?

Management is *people*. Management stresses responsibility; its concern is performance. Management is *organized responsibility*. As Levitt said: "The translation of knowledge into results is almost purely a matter of management." Or this from Drucker: "What makes a manager is responsibility for contribution. It is function rather than power."

What does a manager do?

○ Sets objectives.
○ Organizes.
○ Creates a team—motivates and communicates.
○ Analyzes, appraises, reviews, and interprets performance.
○ Develops people.
○ Acts as a "working boss" rather than as a "coordinator."

The administrative job of the manager is to optimize

the yield from available resources. Thinking things up is not the same as making things happen.

Risk taking is of the essence. It is better to make an error of commission than an error of omission. *Action* is the key word. Management is not standing still but acting and reacting, moving ever forward.

Flexibility—never rigidity—is the key. A good manager gets his people to do more work than anyone else can—and do it willingly.

While we need to be efficient (to do things well), we also need to be concerned with effectiveness. Drucker would have us ask: Are we doing the *right* things to achieve our goals? Are we doing what we do best? Are we doing what is most profitable for us to do?

Our entire effort is directed at having customers and clients *prefer* to do business with us. This effort must be clear, and our purpose must be sound. An enterprise needs to offer its patrons an advantage that will gain it preference. It needs to build a strategy around this advantage, to create a niche for itself so it can withstand competition. It is the responsibility of management to develop both the advantage and the strategy for gaining the preference.

THE MANAGER AS PROBLEM SOLVER

One of the most important ongoing functions of a manager, at any level, is that of problem solver. This, of course, involves the ability to uncover problems. It is not enough to deal with problems after they have become major crises. Managerial skill lies in the ability to uncover problems in the incipient stage, when they are small and easy to solve. Later on we will discuss observation and review, two aspects of the eternal search for little problems which, when dealt with promptly, enable us to avoid crises.

Problem solving requires a close interpersonal relationship with subordinates. The manager who isolates himself behind his desk will learn too late of problems. The tiny flame will be a conflagration by the time he discovers it. On the other hand, the manager who periodically reviews progress with a subordinate will hear things that, to his sophisticated ear, suggest a possible problem—one that his subordinate may have overlooked or considered of little importance at the moment.

THE IMPORTANCE OF STRUCTURE IN AN ORGANIZATION

Lyndall F. Urwick likens the organization chart to the electrical plan of a large building. Each little block indicating an employee and his job is a point through which messages pass like electrical energy. If that point is disconnected, nothing can flow through it in either direction.

Each manager is such a connector. It is his function to communicate down to those under him, and through them to those to whom they must communicate on such matters as policy, operating rules, product and pricing information, and corporate image (what the organization stands for). He must also communicate upward to management on such issues as customer reaction, product acceptance or rejection in the marketplace, employee satisfactions or dissatisfactions, and operating improvements.

The principles of good structure include:

1. Clarity—each person knows his job and how it relates to other jobs.
2. Economy—there is minimum effort to control, supervise, and perform.

3

Figure 1. Organization structures.

A DETAILED CHART

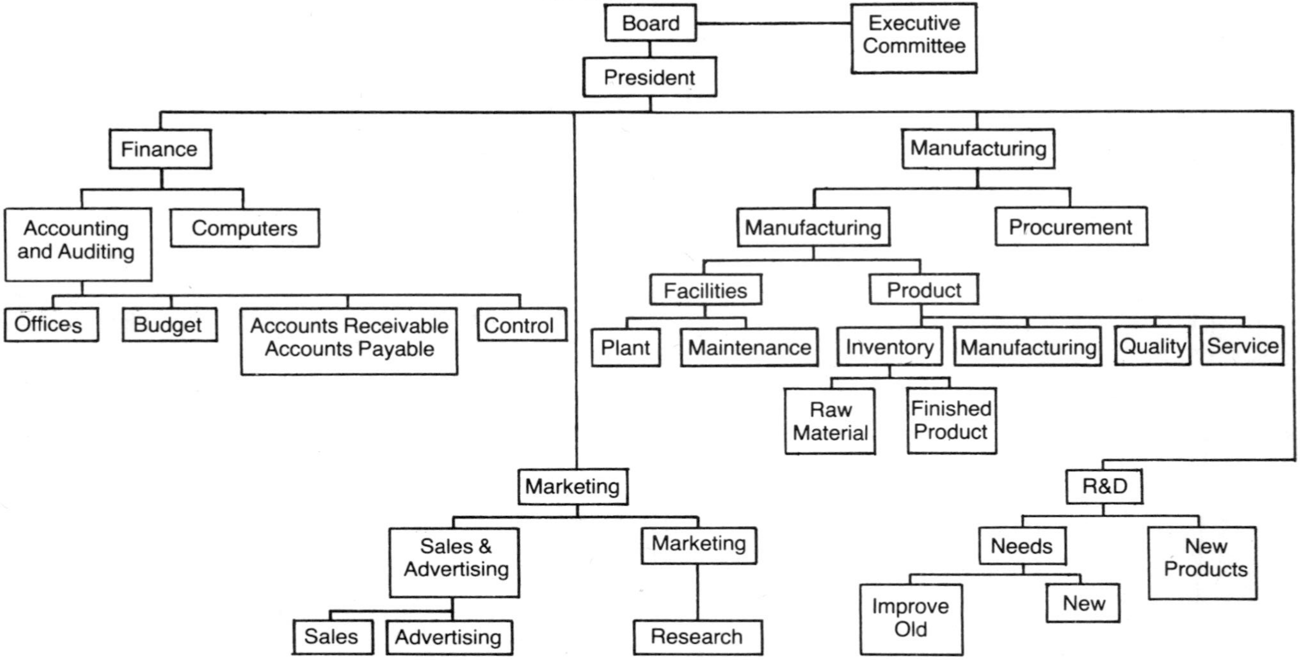

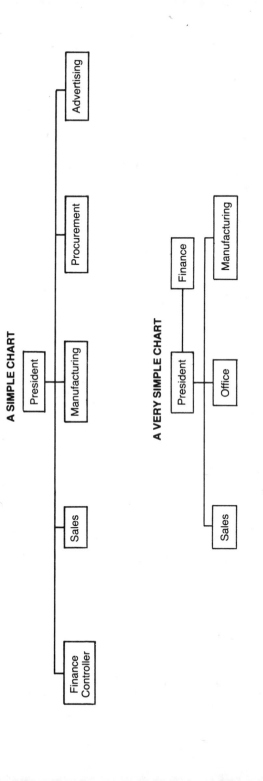

A SIMPLE CHART

President

Finance Controller | Sales | Manufacturing | Procurement | Advertising

A VERY SIMPLE CHART

President

Finance

Sales | Office | Manufacturing

3. Performance—structure keeps people focused on performing.
4. Ease of decision making.
5. Adaptability and flexibility.
6. Development of new leadership—structure points up where it is needed.

There is no best structure. A structure must be built around organizational needs and objectives. It should be simple, with a minimum number of echelons. Top management must be able to see the entire operation. Out of this should come a management team—a planning and review group whose members have broad authority within their areas of accountability.

Figures 1 and 2 are examples (and only examples) of

Figure 2. Making MBO work.

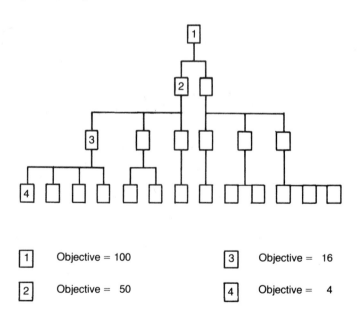

| 1 | Objective = 100 | 3 | Objective = 16 |
| 2 | Objective = 50 | 4 | Objective = 4 |

how to structure an organization and how to use organization charts as management tools.

In Figure 2 the process is as follows. Managers 1 and 2 in conference agree that 2 will accept an objective of 50. Then 2 and 3 in conference agree that 3 will accept an objective of 16. Then 3 and 4 in conference agree that 4 will accept an objective of 4. (The objective is discussed and then agreed upon. It is measurable and attainable. The agreement is a *commitment* to reach the objective.)

In the supervisory process, the manager reviews performance toward objectives with his subordinate (1 reviews with 2; 2 reviews with 3; 3 reviews with 4). The results of the reviews are plans for action to reach agreed-upon objectives. Problems are analyzed and solutions developed. Obstacles are removed. The manager helps his subordinate through observing his methods and counseling with him.

The results of this process are communicated upward so that accurate information on progress toward objectives is continually flowing to higher echelons. Thus any problems or obstacles are quickly uncovered and solutions found. Forward movement toward objectives continues unabated.

Management must have rules by which people operate and interrelate. In Figure 3, each manager must know the extent of his authority. When 2 and 3 have a conflict that they cannot resolve themselves within company policy, they take the problem to 1. When 4 and 5 have a conflict that they cannot resolve themselves, each takes the problem to his immediate superior—to 2 and 3 respectively. If 2 and 3 cannot resolve it, the problem goes to 1. When 2 and 5 are in conflict, they take the problem to 3. If it cannot be resolved by 3, it goes to 1.

Sometimes interrelationships have never been clarified

Figure 3. Reporting structures for resolving a conflict.

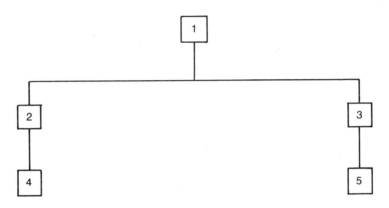

and can cause conflict. For example, managers 4 and 5 may be working on the same project at the same time. In this kind of situation immediate clarification of responsibility is important.

When two people work on a project together or with a third person, it should be clear which person has overall responsibility. It is good management to always place single, final responsibility with one person. For instance, if managers 4 and 5 work together and the final responsibility lies with 4, any conflict that cannot be resolved must go to 2, who is the superior of 4. If 5 is unhappy, he can take the matter to 3, his superior, who will then go to 2 and attempt to resolve the matter.

EVALUATING RESOURCES: PEOPLE AND MONEY

Resources must be evaluated continually to make sure that they are being used to the fullest and to make sure that management is not attempting to do more than it has the resources to do. Two important resources are *people* and *money*.

PEOPLE EVALUATION

1. What people do you have now?
   - What can they contribute?
   - Which ones can be part of the management team?
   - Which ones should be replaced . When can this be done without disrupting operations? ("Never throw out dirty water until you have clean.")
2. What slots are unfilled?
   - Can you afford to fill the slots now, or will you need to wait?
   - Do you have the right person? Can this person be spared, or will the promotion just create another vacant spot?
   - What must be invested in finding and training the right person so that the job can be performed without supervision? (Consider the total cost until the job is paying its way.)
3. What is your entire responsibility? Which functions will you perform yourself? To whom will you delegate the remaining functions?
   - Do you have the people? How will you deploy them?
   - Do you have the people to carry on the day-to-day operations while the new or improved operations are getting under way?

The entire operation must go on, must be profitable, must achieve objectives. Make sure the people are available to do this.

MONEY EVALUATION

1. Are financial resources adequate to carry on present plans and objectives? If not, what can be done about it?

2. Every echelon should have a budget. Every manager should know what financial resources are available to him. What money can he spend without approval from his superior?

3. To the extent that the following are applicable, the manager should consider the finances necessary for wages and salaries, raw materials, funds for meeting accounts payable promptly, sales and marketing expenses, reserves for carrying slow accounts, funds for settling complaints or rejects, taxes, rent, inventory, and the like.

4. If a new venture is planned, there must be adequate funds to see the venture through. Never start what you cannot finish.

5. Financial planning should include the building of reserves:

 ○ For new ideas, product testing, and new markets.
 ○ For adding to staff.
 ○ For modern equipment to maintain productivity.

6. Financial planning should involve—at the top—consultation with bankers, attorneys, and accountants as well as in-organization personnel with special skills.

Remember that good managers evaluate continually. An ounce of foresight is worth more than a pound of hindsight.

MULTILATERAL CONSULTATION

Decision making calls for extreme caution. An important decision can have far-reaching effects. The greatest danger lies in the head of an organization making decisions unilaterally. Two or three heads are better than one. Critical decisions should be made in consultation with a number of qualified people, in whom top management has great confidence. In a small organization a decision-making group should be formed, advisory to top management, consisting of an attorney, an accountant, and a banker. This group may include top inside people. Their involvement will add another dimension to decision making, helping to motivate them, and give them a commitment to the decisions made. In addition to carrying out the job assigned, these people become valuable contributors to good management.

When one or two people dominate in an organization, the "consulting group" approach brings fresh thinking to management and removes blocks to sound decision making.

THE PRINCIPLE OF HIGHEST SKILL

No person should perform any task that can be performed just as well by someone who is paid less. This principle applies to all echelons insofar as possible.

How to employ this principle: *Identify your highest skill and devote your time to performing it. Delegate all other skills.*

Delegation is not abdication, nor is it "breathing down another's neck." Give responsibility to others. But remember that the delegated work is part of your job, so you must review performance regularly to make sure that problems are being resolved and work is moving forward toward objectives.

Put instructions in writing. Delegate jobs that can be done just as well or even better by someone who is paid less than you, or who is capable of being trained to do the job as well.

Why delegate? So that you can perform at your highest skill and thus be of maximum value to the organization. You should not be saddled with jobs below your level of competence. To be relaxed about delegating responsibilities you should give those who report to you *very specific tasks* and teach them how to perform those tasks. Training and development is aimed at having those under the manager perform assigned tasks at least as well as the manager himself.

Motivate those to whom work is delegated. Listen. Respect others' opinions and judgments. Encourage decision making on their part. Ask: "What would *you* do?" Help, advise, and counsel. Then pat people on the back for a job well done.

DELEGATION TO A SECRETARY OR ADMINISTRATIVE ASSISTANT

To perform at highest skill, a manager must have someone to relieve him of the details of his job. This person may be a part-time employee assigned to one or more managers. Or it may be an administrative assistant or a full-time secretary (not a stenographer/file clerk but someone much better qualified). In any case, it is the responsibility of the manager to *train* his assistant to perform the delegated tasks. (For a partial list of the kinds of tasks to be delegated, see Chapter 6.)

Delegation must be explicit. In the following example, Joe is being "thrown to the wolves" in the illustration of the wrong way. His superior will probably blame him for failure to do what was expected, and Joe will be a disgruntled employee who feels he has had a raw deal. In the illustration of the right way, Joe knows exactly what is expected of him. Without being told, he knows whether he is doing well or not. He and his superior are a team working together. Joe is happy and proud of the responsibility placed in him. He is very likely to succeed.

Delegating the wrong way:

"Joe, I want you to take over the department and run it. I'll be in touch with you. I know you can do it."

Delegating the right way:

"Joe, I want you to take over the department. Here are the main requirements:

1. The department must turn out no less than 275 units a day.
2. The department must not have more than 5 percent· rejects.
3. You must develop at least one promotable person this year.
4. Here are the union rules to be followed.
5. I will meet with you every Monday morning at ten in my office to help you in any way.
6. Do you have any questions now?
7. I'll send you these items in a memo."

2

The Cycle
of Management

Good managers know what they must do and how to go about doing it. They know how to get people of ordinary ability to perform in an extraordinary manner. They can get more work and better performance from those under them, and get this willingly.

People must want to do what the manager is trying to get them to do. This is achieved by continually operating within the Cycle of Management. What is the Cycle? Let's go over each step quickly. (We'll consider each one in depth in later chapters.)

STEP 1: PLANNING

Planning involves three stages:

1. Setting objectives that are agreed upon, measurable, and attainable.

2. Determining how to reach them—developing a strategy.
3. Setting a timetable for reaching the objectives.

Planning must be flexible. It must allow for change but represent the best current thinking. Planning is best done through a team (a person and his immediate superior). A plan for a subordinate is more likely to be carried out if it is set by a manager and the subordinate. When a person is involved in the planning process, he feels a commitment to achieving objectives.

STEP 2: PERFORMING THE ACTION PLANNED

From a management point of view, performance involves getting the right people to carry out the plans and making sure the plans are achieved.

Give the plans a chance. When a manager constantly changes his plans, the result is chaos. Subordinates are frustrated, and morale is bad. People lose confidence in the manager. There is a time to consider whether any changes should be made—and that is step 3.

STEP 3: APPRAISING PROGRESS TOWARD OBJECTIVES

Appraisal is a critical step in the cycle—the point where the manager and his team pause in their efforts and ask themselves: "How are we doing?" This question is asked only in terms of the objectives ("How are we doing against the objectives we agreed upon, nothing else?")

This is the time to confirm the original planning and strategy or to amend, delete, or add to objectives. This is the time to make sure that the program is moving forward according to plan. The operation will never get out of hand if appraisal is regularly and thoroughly conducted.

STEP 4: DETERMINING WHAT TO DO NEXT AND HOW TO DO IT BETTER

At step 4 in the cycle, management determines the *action* to be taken to keep moving toward objectives. Out of this step must come a clear and agreed-upon understanding of the *next step*, which must be fed back immediately into step 1 to produce better planning. Thus the cycle can continue.

The Cycle of Management repeats itself. If one of the four steps is omitted, the cycle stops. As long as the manager keeps the cycle going, he is continually revitalizing his efforts and insuring the achievement of objectives.

Now we are ready to consider these functions in depth.

3

Planning

Planning is the first step in good management—the first step in the Cycle of Management. The manager has planned well when:

1. In consultation with his immediate superior, he has set agreed-upon objectives to be attained by a specific date and has charted a course of action for achieving those objectives.

2. In consultation with the manager, each subordinate has agreed upon objectives to be attained by a specific date and has determined a course of action for achieving those objectives.

ALLOTTING TIME FOR THE PLANNING PROCESS

Management must allow ample time for the planning process. Planning is often rushed and then squeezed into a short period. Those involved are tense and under pressure.

You can depend on it: This kind of planning will be poorly thought out and poorly executed.

Time should be allotted well in advance for planning. Those involved should have plenty of notice and should have available to them all materials and tools they need. They should arrange their schedules so that there will be no interruptions during the planning session. People should arrive on time and not leave the session while it is in progress. The session should continue until a final plan is developed and ready for implementation.

It is difficult for top management to do much meaningful planning until a series of planning meetings has been held at lower echelons. Planning should start at the bottom of an organization. Two or more people—a person and the person to whom he reports—talk and plan together. Each echelon "guess-estimates" a realistic objective for the year ahead—in terms of what *it* can do.

As the process moves upward, it gathers together the thinking and planning of all echelons of management. At the very top, the various estimates are evaluated and coordinated so that a single plan is developed for the organization. This means that some of the estimates made at lower echelons will need to be revised in the interest of the organization. The final decisions are made at the top, and the reasoning is communicated all the way down to ensure acceptance and wholehearted support.

To repeat: All echelons of management are involved in planning, at three stages. (See Figure 4.)

1. At the lowest echelon the manager and his people "guess-estimate" what they feel they can achieve in the period ahead. This is delivered to the echelon immediately above, which goes through the same process. In this way planning moves progressively upward through the organization.

Figure 4. Corporate planning, stages 1 and 2.

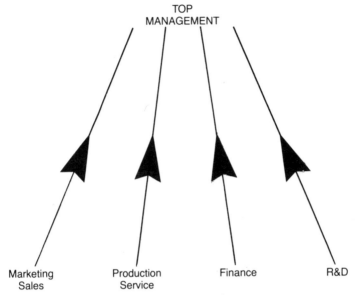

Stage 1: The organization communicates its estimates

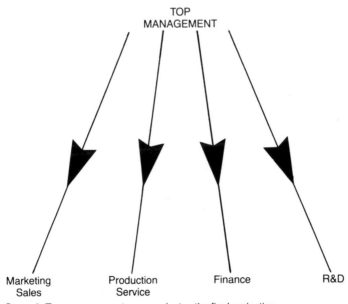

Stage 2: Top management communicates the final projection

Figure 5. Corporate planning, stage 3: 1 million units to be manufactured and sold.

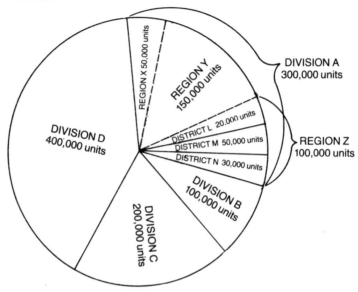

2. After top management has digested all the estimates and added its own best judgments to them, the final plan is developed and handed down through the organization. Each echelon agrees to commit itself to a share of the total. Thus the total objectives are divided among the various echelons and every manager has a part to play. There is total commitment. (See Figure 5.)

3. The manager brings his people together and works with them individually on specific planning. Subobjectives are set within those handed down. Objectives are divided through the entire organization with each manager accepting a portion of the total. This "pie theory" gives each

manager, no matter what his echelon, a sense of responsibility for performing a part of the total corporate job. It also impels him to better performance and raises his morale.

In Figure 5, for example, the corporate goal is 1 million units. Division A accepts 300,000 of the total, and each of the other divisions accepts a share. Within each division are regions, and Division A has been broken down to show how each regional manager accepts a piece of the total. Each region in turn is broken down into districts, and Region Z is shown as an example. Note how each district manager accepts a part of the regional total. All other divisions are broken down similarly.

Before we consider each stage of planning in depth, let's pause to make sure we are all on track. Remember, a manager should be working to achieve some objectives that will move the organization toward a stronger, sounder position. Whether the manager is in sales, production, finance, or administration, he should be going someplace, not just grinding out a static job.

Keep in mind too that planning starts with a review of the present situation. For example:

○ What are the areas of greatest achievement? Why?
○ What are the areas of slow achievement or retrogression? Why?
○ Which operations should be continued and which discontinued? Why?
○ What gaps exist? What should be done about them?
○ What needs stand out?
○ What can be learned for use in planning over the period ahead?

Now let's look more closely at the process.

STAGE 1: SETTING OBJECTIVES

Top management will, of course, set the overall objectives. Drucker suggests eight key areas:

Marketing. What do we want to sell? What does the customer want to buy?

Innovation. Where do we go from here?

People. How can we develop promotable people?

Money. Do we have the money to maintain operations and good credit?

Facilities. Are they adequate?

Productivity. Can we deliver what we sell? Can we produce quality as well as quantity?

Service responsibility. How can we satisfy our customers and minimize complaints?

Profit requirements. Will profits provide funds for growth, reserves, dividends?

In the lower echelons the objectives will vary. For instance, in sales management the objectives for a district manager may be as follows:

o Total sales of the district shall be at least $____.

o All territories shall be filled with productive salesmen.

o All key accounts shall have increased sales of at least ____ percent.

o At least 50 new accounts shall be opened in the district.

o District expenses shall be kept within ____ percent of last year's.

o All key accounts shall buy all product lines.

o Salesmen shall contact each major account at least twice a year.

o At least one promotable salesman shall be developed during the year.

Note that the objectives in the example above are *measurable*. They must be measurable so that the manager knows when an objective has been achieved and the subordinate knows—without being told—whether he is reaching his objective on schedule. Can you imagine a football game where the ten-yards-in-four-downs requirement did not apply?

Objectives must also be *attainable*. Everyone must believe that they can be achieved. Unrealistic objectives are useless. They do harm rather than good. Difficult but realistic objectives provide a challenge and make the manager "stretch" to achieve them. As long as he is willing to commit himself, the objectives are sound.

An objective must not hamstring a manager. It must not tell him *how* to achieve. He must be free to develop his own procedures. Again, to use the example of a football game: The quarterback is restricted only by the ten-yards-in-four-downs rule. Within that, he is free to call any play he wishes, and he can change the original plan if necessary. For instance, he will call a very different play if he is faced with third down and a foot to go, as against third down and 25 yards to go. In the same way, the manager must be free to operate within his area of responsibility, as long as he achieves his objectives.

New directions should be kept within budget. Present operations, even if unsatisfactory, must at least "hold the fort" until new efforts and directions are set under way. Never neglect the ongoing operation and get carried away with the grand scheme.

OBJECTIVES: A DAY-TO-DAY OPERATING TOOL. The manager must live day to day with the objectives to which he is committed. He should have a folder for each objective in his desk drawer and regularly review its contents. He should continually take action and develop the next step in his march toward each objective. *He should never let any objective lie fallow.* After all, he is an integral part of a total effort to achieve the organization's goal. (We will deal with this subject at length in Chapter 6.)

Objectives must be specific, never general. Here is an example:

General	*Specific*
Keep expenses down.	Expenses shall be no more than 3 percent over the previous year.
Increase sales.	
Open more accounts.	
Watch inventory.	Sales shall be increased 15 percent over the previous year.
	Each salesman shall open not less than 6 new accounts.
	Inventory shall not exceed $2 million.

STAGE 2: DETERMINING HOW TO REACH EACH OBJECTIVE

The manager must have a plan—a strategy for achieving each objective. This strategy is best developed in conference with a manager and his immediate superior. Together they discuss such questions as these:

- What obstacles are there to reaching this objective? What can we do about them? We must find some solution worth trying.
- Do we have the right people? Are we trying to do a big

job with little people? We must do something specific to strengthen our manpower situation.

o Do we have the proper tools to do the job? If not, what can we do about it? We must agree on action to be taken.

o Are we going about the job in the best possible way? What are the alternatives?

o Can we agree on controls to make sure we do not get off track? How often should we review the operation together? Our joint input should accelerate our progress and help us work together to resolve incipient crises.

When the two managers have agreed upon (1) measurable, attainable objectives and (2) a strategy to attain them, they should put everything in writing. This written plan is the most important working tool for both managers. It is a guide to the manager who has accepted the objectives as well as a guide to the superior's efforts—a concise statement of what is expected of his subordinate. It shows him where he must assist the subordinate "over the humps."

When a manager accepts objectives, works toward their achievement, and succeeds, he is a good manager. When his superior assists him so that his progress is accelerated and his success is greater than expected, the superior has performed his function.

The entire management function revolves around accepted objectives and the strategy for reaching them.

STAGE 3: SETTING A TIMETABLE FOR ACHIEVING OBJECTIVES

The final stage in good planning is determining when objectives are to be achieved. Against this final date must be some interim evaluation of progress. A series of dates should be set (monthly, quarterly, or whatever is appropriate), and the project should be measured against these "partial objectives." This interim measurement enables management to catch any slippage or problem and do something about it before it becomes serious. All good planning must have a timetable.

Thus we start out with a manageable organization. Every manager knows his job, and those to whom he is accountable know specifically what he is committed to. In this way, the manager can assist those who report to him. There is no reason for any capable manager to fail. The team approach will pick up problems quickly and resolve them before they become crises. The management job is supervisable.

The job of the manager is to help those for whom he is responsible reach their objectives. He is a helper more than a "boss."

Some say that it is best to give a subordinate a job and then leave him alone. But it must be kept in mind that the job given the subordinate is actually part of the manager's own job, for which he is accountable. The principle here is that as long as a manager acts as a counselor and does not interfere in the operations of a subordinate, he can be effective. The team concept need not destroy the subordinate's initiative or sense of responsibility.

The manager should not tell his subordinate how to do something, but rather should stimulate the thinking of the subordinate, provide him with alternate methods to consider, discuss the possible effects of a decision, and finally let the subordinate make the decision himself. He should not be a crutch to lean on, but rather a filter through which good thinking can pass.

As noted earlier, it is important to catch problems before they get out of hand. Regular review of an operation by two echelons of management, working together as a team, is well justified for this reason alone. Well, someone may say, all that is fine. But suppose we find that the objectives are not sound or that the strategy is not working. Do we just keep on going as planned? The answer, of course, is no. Step 3 in the Cycle of Management resolves this common problem. (See Chapters 5 and 6.)

MANPOWER PLANNING

When the manager has completed the planning sessions with his people, he can assess fairly accurately (1) his manpower requirements and (2) the manpower potential in his area of responsibility. At this point he knows which of his people are capable of development—of being promoted— and which are not.

A good manager will not tolerate inadequate people. When an employee's performance is unsatisfactory and he does not appear to be capable of development, a determination must be made.

- Should the employee be replaced immediately?
- What if the employee is an older person or in ill health?
  Should he be retired and then replaced?
  Should he be assigned a smaller responsibility?
  Should his work be divided with another?
  Should he be transferred or reassigned?
- Can the employee be used elsewhere and therefore be transferred?
- Should an assistant or trainee be assigned to this person, with a view to later replacement?
- Should a replacement be sought at once and the old employee kept on until the new person is trained?

Thus the manager can determine how many new people will be needed to make sure that objectives are reached. The manager's manpower estimates should be a part of his planning with his immediate superior. In any event, the workforce must be kept at full strength to produce the commitments embodied in the objectives.

To add it all up: Good planning doesn't try to accomplish more than is possible. It involves a balancing of all elements in the operation. Planning is a team job. It involves many people and their assessment of realistic goals to be accomplished. It represents a commitment on the part of every member of management to perform a specific part of the job.

Good planning produces healthy, steady growth throughout the organization—because it is participatory. When people achieve their objectives, they are confident and happy and will try to do even better the next time around. Thus the organization is healthy and successful; customers are satisfied and well serviced. *All echelons of management feel that they have played a part in the achievement. And they are right.*

When planning has been completed, implementation begins at once—a topic we turn to in the following chapter.

ADDENDUM: ACCOUNT DEVELOPMENT AS A PLANNING TOOL *

Peter Drucker says that the purpose of business is to create a customer. And, we might add, to hold and develop that customer. The cost of creating, retaining, and developing a

* Most readers will find the concept of account development useful in their operations. For certain organizations, however, this concept does not apply. The idea is well worth presenting for those who find it helpful.

customer is so great today that many organizations have found it highly profitable to be selective in determining who their customers will be. To go after customers willy-nilly may produce losses rather than gains.

Consider not only the actual cost of selling the account initially but also the cost of servicing the account and helping the account obtain maximum results from the product or service sold. Consider too the cost of educating the account—training it in the area of the seller's special expertise. Clearly, we are talking about the expenditure of a great deal of employee time—our most costly commodity—plus considerable money.

In most organizations, approximately 80 percent of the potential business is derived from about 20 percent of the potential buyers. Each enterprise must find out who comprises that 20 percent of potential buyers. This group must be sold—or a considerable number of them sold. It pays to make the effort to sell them, because their purchases are profitable. This is where the business *is*. This is where the effort must be made. (Note: Some local enterprises may deliberately abdicate business to larger competitors while devoting their time to serving smaller accounts in their area. But even in this situation they soon find it necessary to become selective in choosing customers.)

Once an enterprise has identified and isolated the 20 percent of potential customers who can provide 80 percent of the potential business, it should make that information part of the entire operating strategy of the organization. The sales department will need to know where to concentrate its efforts. The advertising people will need to know where to concentrate their advertising. In addition, the manufacturing divisions will need to know what kind of product customers want. The service departments will need to know what kind of service is required, what kind of delivery is expected, how to deal with complaints, and how to handle special requests, billing, and credit matters. The research and development people will want to know customers' needs. *The modern organization is market-oriented from top to bottom.*

No one can argue against the importance of account development as a tool of sales management. Every good salesman will make a major effort to sell the "target" or "key" accounts—the 20 percent that can provide 80 percent of the potential business. Since sales costs are so high (salaries or other compensation, expenses, fringe benefits, and the like), management is concerned more with account coverage than with territorial coverage. In fact, geographical territories are zoned around clusters of target or key accounts. Primary attention is paid to planning calls and securing business from them. Since worthwhile smaller accounts are often located near the larger accounts, these "satellite" accounts are called on when a salesperson is visiting a major account in the area. The salesman who devotes a large portion of his time and effort to important accounts needs the full force of the organization behind him in order to provide the kind of service that will make the account prefer to deal with him. So the idea of account development as a tool of general management has some merit.

When the entire organization is market-oriented, everybody—from the loader on the shipping dock to the stenographer and bookkeeper—must understand and work toward satisfying the customer's needs. Such an orientation involves planning at the top level. The principle should be communicated through the entire organization, with the full backing of all echelons of management.

Definition of an important (key or target) account: any account with sufficiently large volume and profitability, on a continuing basis, to justify giving it service superior to what any competitor gives. The goal is to make the customer prefer to do business with the organization giving this superior service. It is this preference that gives an organization the edge—the potential for greater growth and greater profitability.

When management has isolated the important accounts, it can develop a strategy for obtaining a major share of the business of each account. If the account is presently being sold, the strategy will revolve around increasing sales. If the account has never been or is not presently being sold, the strategy will revolve around initiating business. Managers in areas other than sales can be involved in developing the strategy and indeed often are in many organizations.

Specific product lines or products can be studied to develop a strategy for introducing them to important, high-volume accounts. One of the greatest advantages of having the entire organization involved in specific accounts is that sales slippages can be easily isolated and management can obtain reliable answers to why volume has declined. In many instances, the organization can then find a way to restore profitable volume.

4

Implementation

To implement a plan, the manager must have the right subordinates to help him perform the job. He must also supervise, instruct, and counsel subordinates to help them reach their objectives. The objectives agreed upon by the manager and his subordinates become the *plan of action* for the manager, and of course for the subordinates.

The job of the manager is to help subordinates reach their objectives. This is how the manager attains his own objectives and helps the organization reach its objectives.

The real test of good management is the ability to implement plans successfully. The greatest single obstacle to successful management by objectives (MBO) lies in failing to carry out the operations needed to achieve objectives. Often, an organization gets excited about MBO and gets everybody involved in setting agreed-upon objectives. But then the objectives are forgotten. It is implementation that counts.

Management must have continuity. Implementation cannot be a series of unrelated activities. Too often a manager says to himself, "I'd better check up on Barbara and see how she is doing." Or, "I haven't been with Joe for a while. I'd better go down to see him." Implementation is a process, a series of planned, agreed-upon actions developed by a manager and his subordinate. Let us see how this works.

The manager should spend time with the subordinate *where* the subordinate is working. It is important that the manager see the subordinate in action. Such contacts should be well planned and should take place at regular intervals. The manager will determine what the intervals will be and may narrow or widen them as he sees fit. The schedule need not be the same for all subordinates. Some will need to be contacted more often than others.

The purpose of these contacts is to improve the subordinate's performance and accelerate his progress toward his objectives. The planned contacts involve three highly important steps: (1) Observation, (2) Review, and (3) Action. Let us discuss each of these in turn.

OBSERVATION

How can a manager help his subordinates if he has not seen them in action? Certainly not from any written reports. Only by observing can the manager know for certain what is being done well and what weaknesses call for his help. Without observation, the manager may be "losing" his subordinate: by criticizing what need not be criticized; by trying to teach where the subordinate already excels; by failing to help where help is desperately needed. Observation reveals whether the subordinate is learning what is being taught, whether he is trying to learn but having trouble, whether he cannot break his old habits, and whether he really wants to do what the manager is telling him to do.

·If the manager has observed carefully, he can use his time with the subordinate to correct weaknesses and get him back on track, moving toward his objectives. Thus the contact results in the immediate correction of a problem.

FORMS OF OBSERVATION. It may be difficult to imagine how a subordinate can be observed while he is functioning in his job. Observation can be awkward or uncomfortable, and some finesse may be required. It is not a policing action. The subordinate must realize that observation is the best way to get help. Experience has indicated that high performers welcome observation because it shows their superior how good they are. Poor performers try to avoid observation because it exposes their weaknesses.

Here are a few ways in which observation can be carried out:

- A sales manager observes a salesman while he is calling on a customer.
- A regional sales manager observes a district sales manager by traveling with him for a day when he is with one of his salesmen.
- A manager in a manufacturing operation observes a subordinate out in the plant as he supervises his employees.
- A manager in the office or accounting area observes a subordinate manager while he is overseeing workers.
- A manager observes a subordinate, not in front of the job but as part of the review conference.

Observation gives the manager firsthand knowledge of the work of the subordinate, not for the purpose of policing but for the purpose of improving performance. Managerial skills are thus put to work where they are most needed and can do the most good.

REVIEW

Review is the management tool that tells whether progress is being made. The manager and his subordinate have agreed on certain steps to be taken. Did the subordinate take these steps? Have his efforts resulted in improved performance? Are the agreed-upon objectives being attained?

The review is really a two-way discussion around these questions. If a problem exists, the manager will ferret out the causes and work to overcome them. The review is an indication of the subordinate's willingness to improve his performance. Has he tried hard to do what he agreed to do? The review often tells the manager whether the subordinate is a good investment.

The review should not become a "report" by the subordinate to the manager. A report suggests that the manager is policing the job, and the subordinate is likely to be defensive, since reporting will be more personal and deal with him. The review is a team operation—two people talking together about the job. It is oriented to the job and to objectives. "How are we doing in reaching *our* objectives?" is a different kind of query from "How are *you* doing?" The review provides an opportunity for the manager to work effectively with subordinates.

ACTION

Action must always result from observation and review. The manager and his subordinate agree on action to be taken by the subordinate—usually before the next scheduled contact with the manager. This agreement represents a commitment by the subordinate to improve his performance in the areas covered during the review. The action is put into writing (see Figure 6), and the subsequent work of the subordinate provides an accurate measure of his ability and willingness to grow in his work.

The real test of the subordinate is how well he can perform what he agreed to do. When the subordinate has

---

Figure 6. Contact and review record.

Name of employee _____

Date _____

1. What was done at this contact or review?

2. What does the employee do very well?

3. In what areas is there room for improvement?

4. What action was taken to improve performance?

5. What action is to be taken between this date and the date of the next contact or review?

6. When will the next contact or review take place?

7. Other comments:

Name of manager _____

Figure 7. How observation and review are translated into action to improve the performance of subordinates.

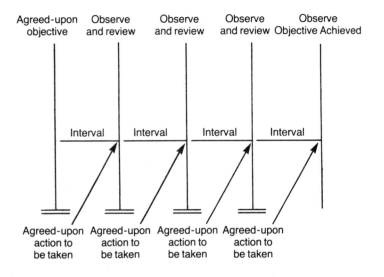

Note: Each vertical line represents a contact between manager and subordinate on the job.

learned, the objective will be achieved. (See Figure 7.) Remember, the sum of the objectives of all subordinates equals the manager's objectives.

MISTAKES THAT DILUTE A MANAGER'S EFFECTIVENESS

1. The manager tries to manage from behind his desk. It can't be done. The manager sees only "the numbers," not the manner in which the job is being tackled, the way the subordinate handles those who report to him, or the ability of the subordinate to see problems and deal with them quickly.

2. The manager spends time with his subordinate on

minor matters or nitpicking and never gets around to observing work toward objectives.

3. The manager draws erroneous conclusions about a subordinate. This not only is unfair to the subordinate but can hurt the manager's chances to reach his own objectives.

4. The manager operates mechanically. For instance, he attempts to instruct a subordinate in an area where the subordinate is already proficient. The manager "loses" the subordinate, who then loses confidence in and respect for him.

5. The manager fails to give a pat on the back when it is deserved.

6. The manager fails to develop a team. He *tells* subordinates what to do and does not obtain agreement on a course of action. He forgets that the subordinate must want to do what the manager feels he should do. The manager is a teacher and should have the subordinate practice sound techniques in his presence so he can perfect the subordinate's work. When the subordinate sees that the improved method works—that it helps him—and realizes that he can perform it on his own, the manager is performing at his highest skill.

CHANGING HABITS

It may appear that personal on-the-job contact between a manager and his subordinates is being overemphasized in these pages. Keep in mind, however, that the manager is attempting to change established habits of his subordinates. He says in effect: "Stop doing it that way and start doing it this way." Even after his subordinates accept this point of view and want to follow his directions, they are in for a very difficult time.

Anyone who has ever tried to stop smoking knows how difficult it is to change fixed habits. Efforts to break habits fail far more frequently than they succeed. We have all heard: "This one cigarette won't hurt me." Such a remark usually signals the defeat of resolve. So the subordinate starts out with every intention of doing what his manager told him to do, but under pressure of the daily job he reverts to his old habits. Unless the subordinate is put back on track promptly, it will become increasingly difficult, if not impossible, to get him back on track later.

The alert manager, therefore, expects backsliding and watches for it. When it appears, he immediately helps the subordinate over the hump. Consequently, the interval between reversions to old habits widens after each effort. Eventually the habit is changed, and the manager initiates further efforts to improve performance.

Figures 8 and 9 illustrate the principles just discussed. In Figure 8, the interval between reversions widens from 1 to 2, 2 to 3, and so forth, until the habit is changed altogether and the manager has achieved the desired result.

Figure 8. Instilling new work habits in subordinates.

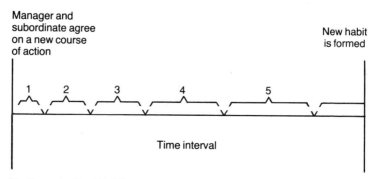

Manager and subordinate agree on a new course of action

New habit is formed

1 2 3 4 5

Time interval

V = Reversion to old habit

Figure 9. The need for catching problems at an early stage.

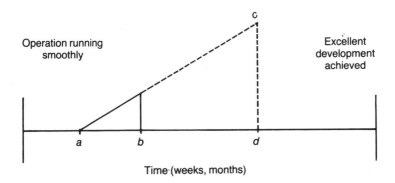

Time·(weeks, months)

In Figure 9, a problem arises at point *a*. If it is handled promptly, it can be resolved and the effort brought back in line at point *b*. If action is neglected until point *c*, the situation may deteriorate so much that achieving point *d* is almost impossible.

THE "OBSERVATION CONTACT" OR ON-THE-JOB CONFERENCE

PLANNING AND PREPARATION

1. Review the agreed-upon objectives. Determine which of these should be the subject of special consideration at this time.
2. Study records of the subordinate's performance to determine where you can be of help.
3. Review your file folder on the subordinate for matters to be discussed or areas calling for improvement.
4. Determine whether there are any special situations requiring your help.

43

5. Determine the length of this contact or conference.

6. If possible, tell the subordinate in advance of your plans and ask him whether there are any matters he wishes to discuss with you or matters he wants you involved in while you are with him. If you involve your subordinate in planning the meeting, the results will be more rewarding.

HINTS FOR CONDUCTING THE CONTACT

1. Start by discussing those matters of greatest importance to the subordinate. Alleviate his concerns so that he is ready to listen.

2. Do not be diverted from the agenda planned for the contact. Diversions usually prevent completion of important items to be covered. Insist on staying with the agenda, except in an emergency.

3. Maintain informality so that it is easy for the subordinate to "open up" about what is on his mind.

4. Be alert to his complaints. It may be the subordinate's way of indicating areas where he needs help.

5. Do not get involved in personal problems of the subordinate unless they affect his performance or the image of the organization. Only then should they become the manager's concern.

6. Do not discuss other personnel—either superiors at any level or peers of the subordinate. No comparisons should be made. This kind of discussion does not improve the performance of the subordinate and may do harm. In any event, it consumes valuable time.

7. Never make a commitment unless you fully expect to carry it out. A sure way to lose the confidence of the

subordinate is to promise something and then fail to deliver.

8. Make sure all your cards are on the table. The subordinate must know exactly where he stands with you. This is sometimes painful but it is rewarding because you will gain the subordinate's trust and respect.

9. Be prepared to take risks by placing responsibility in the subordinate's hands. Risk taking is one of the prime qualities of good management. In most instances, the subordinate will merit the confidence placed in him. Good managers are confident and secure enough to risk letting subordinates take real responsibility in certain circumstances.

At this point some managers may ask: "How can we get our job done if we are away from our desk as much as you recommend?" It is a good question and it is answered in depth in Chapter 6, on control.

Remember that when subordinates are involved in the planning function, they will feel a commitment to carrying out the plans they helped to formulate. In relating to subordinates, the manager can say: "Recall that *you and I* planned the operation that you were to perform. Is there some reason it has not been performed? Have you changed your mind? Give me your thinking."

INTERPERSONAL RELATIONSHIPS

The manager must understand his subordinates and the potential conflicts that may arise. For example:

o An older manager may resent a younger manager. It is hard for a subordinate to "take from" a younger person. He may even feel better qualified than his boss.

○ Former peers of a newly promoted manager may resent the fact that they were not promoted and show their feelings by throwing roadblocks in the way of the manager.

○ Dissatisfactions and gripes often fester under the skin. A good manager brings them to the surface at once, cleans out the wound, and tries to heal it. Discuss such matters openly. Disarm the subordinate with complete frankness at all times. Let him talk it out. Listen, and the subordinate will cooperate more readily.

○ Subordinates must feel that the manager will champion their just cause when he is before top management. They will also respect him for championing the cause of the organization when he is with them.

○ Subordinates must recognize that the manager *is* management.

In all cases, the manager must run a tight ship. He must insist that there be positive movement toward objectives. No excuses. When all is said and done, the organization must move forward and achieve objectives on schedule.

Managers must never forget that successful operations depend on having people who want to do a topnotch job, want to succeed, and want to do what the manager suggests—people who are trying to perform at their best all the time. A good manager cannot afford anything less.

The manager is not a policeman; nor is he a psychiatrist or social worker. He should not try to do what is beyond his ability. It is his job to take capable people and accelerate their development through good supervision and training. Managers must be promotable, and they must have subordinates who are promotable. If the subordinates are themselves managers, it is even more important that they develop at an accelerated pace. Through this process the entire organization grows from within and is strengthened in the important area of manpower.

Implementation involves working directly with subordinates to bring about (1) the achievement of agreed-upon objectives, and (2) the development of a promotable people.

5

Review, Appraisal, and Motivation

REGULARLY SCHEDULED REVIEWS

Every manager accepts "a piece" of his superior's objectives and works toward achieving it. The goal is to build a management team in which each subordinate is obligated to perform a specific task.

Each manager must conduct a regular review of every subordinate to determine whether the job is being done. This review can be made independently or in a conference with the subordinate. The purpose of the review is:

- To examine the subordinate's progress toward agreed-upon objectives.
- To improve the subordinate's performance.
- To confirm, amend, or alter objectives within the manager's authority.
- To provide a measure (from one review to the next) of progress within a definite time span.

○ To ferret out problems in the incipient stage so that they can be resolved quickly.

○ To provide continuity in the appraisal process so that more accurate conclusions can be drawn. This should improve the upward flow of information to management.

Adherence to schedule should have top priority. The manager will decide on the interval between reviews (once a week, once every two weeks, or monthly). But whatever the schedule, it must be maintained. The manager cannot allow other matters to take priority over the review. What is more important than that he know whether his job is being performed?

THE REVIEW CONFERENCE. The manager should try to conduct some reviews in conference with subordinates. Certainly a review conference should be scheduled at least three or four times a year. Such a conference is in reality an exchange of information. An agenda should be circulated in advance to allow time for study and preparation. This process minimizes "off the top of the head" judgments and results in better decision making. And the sessions will be shorter because they will be right on track.

When the review takes the form of a conference between the manager and his subordinate, regular scheduling is especially important. If the conference is repeatedly postponed or delayed because the manager gives priority to other duties, the subordinate will soon conclude that he and his job are not important to his superior.

The review should deal with the specific responsibilities delegated to the subordinate. By keeping within this well-defined framework, the superior avoids time-consuming consideration of minor subjects that dilute the value of the review.

Out of each review should come some *plan of action*—things to be done to improve performance and accelerate movement toward objectives. If the review is held in conference, the action can be decided upon immediately and each of the conferees given a memo on the agreed-upon action. If the review is done independently, any suggestions for action can be conveyed to the subordinate by telephone. The "telephone conference" can be very effective in place of a personal conference *if both parties are prepared for it.*

Some continuity must be built into the review. The manager should regularly read through the various memos on plans of action determined in previous reviews. (See Figure 6 in Chapter 4.) These memos should be kept in the subordinate's folder. Reading through the memos helps the manager evaluate the subordinate's growth and development and indicates whether the action has been carried out and whether certain problem areas persist.

THE MANAGER'S WEEKLY REVIEW. Generally, the manager should conduct some form of weekly review of the work of his subordinates. Such a review involves:

- Looking at the latest statistics on the subordinate's performance.
- Looking through the subordinate's folder to see whether any items require follow-up or special action.
- Looking at records of previous reviews to see if progress has been made.
- Using any other measure of movement toward objectives.

This review should be held at the same time each week and should have high priority. It provides an opportunity to commend a subordinate on his progress or special achievements and to get him back on track immediately if he seems to stray. It gives the manager an in-depth knowledge of the work of the subordinate. Such information is of great value in helping the subordinate toward his objectives.

THE APPRAISAL PROCESS

The purpose of appraisal is to improve performance. Efficient appraisal consists of (1) regular evaluation of the progress made by each subordinate toward agreed-upon objectives; (2) regular evaluation of the manager's progress toward his own objectives; and (3) recognition of the action to be taken to move steadily toward the agreed-upon objectives, the best way to perform this action, and a time schedule for getting it done.

To place appraisal in proper perspective as a vital management function, we should recall that appraisal is the third step in the Cycle of Management. After the manager has observed his subordinates in their work environment, reviewed their performance, and helped them improve their performance, he pauses and takes a long look to determine whether progress is being made. This pause is *appraisal.*

The manager says to himself: "How are we doing? We made plans—set objectives—and tried to carry them out. Now, at this point, are we moving toward our objectives at the right speed?" Here the manager is looking at the subordinate and himself—the team—as well as at the subordinate individually. But he should not forget that the purpose of his appraisal is to gauge progress toward objectives—not personalities.

Appraisal cannot take place in a vacuum. It is a form of

measurement. Performance must be evaluated against some valid objectives. Other factors may need to be evaluated, but they should be considered minor compared with objectives. There is nothing unusual about this fact. In tennis, the ultimate objective is the match, but there are lesser objectives—points, and sets—which tell the player how well he is doing in achieving his major objective.

Appraisal is a continuous process. Wake a manager in the middle of the night and he can tell you who his best people are. Managers are continually thinking about their people, about the job to be done, and about their progress or lack of it. But one important factor must be understood. Appraisal is of no value unless it is discussed with the subordinate. Like a medical examination, its value lies in sharing the diagnosis with the patient and agreeing upon a course of action.

This discussion—or any discussion of a subordinate's performance with him—is called *counseling*. It may be just a pat on the back or an effort to correct a weakness. Every subordinate is anxious to know how his manager views his performance—and he wants to hear directly from his boss. Skillful appraisal and counseling can improve a subordinate's attitude and performance. They can keep him on track and speed his progress. Counseling is effective if the subordinate recognizes and accepts it as a way of helping him.

There are two kinds of appraisal: informal and formal. *Informal appraisal* is the ongoing, day-to-day appraisal by the manager. *Formal appraisal* is the annual or semiannual in-depth appraisal that involves filling out a formal printed form sent out by headquarters. The appraisal form can vary from a single sheet of paper to a lengthy document, depending on the degree of detail required by management. As someone said: it is quite FORMidable.

53

Both types of appraisal deal with three factors: (1) actual progress toward objectives, which considers results; (2) methods employed in achieving results; and (3) personal characteristics of the subordinate—strengths, weaknesses, and promotability. Let us consider each type of appraisal briefly.

INFORMAL APPRAISAL. The manager is constantly appraising his work and that of his subordinates. His superiors are anxious to know what progress he and his team are making. The manager is continually looking at the ability of each subordinate to carry his share of the load. And the subordinate wants to know what his superior thinks of his performance.

The accurate appraisal of a subordinate depends on careful observation. Of course, the manager counsels and appraises each time he is with a subordinate. The meeting may take only ten minutes, but it brings the manager and his subordinate closer together. When skillfully conducted, appraisal gives the subordinate the feeling that he is helping the manager. He and his manager should agree on the next steps to be taken, and the agreement should be put into a written memo for both.

FORMAL APPRAISAL. Formal appraisal provides a means of standardizing the company's appraisal procedure. Through it, higher echelons are able to analyze the performance of subordinates as far down the line as they wish to go. This may be valuable for filling openings from time to time. No matter how cleverly the form is prepared, in the last analysis what matters is how it is completed. If the form is filled out carelessly or inaccurately, the entire appraisal is worthless. It can do harm to the people involved and to the organization.

There are many kinds of appraisal. In some organizations, the subordinate performs self-appraisal, and his superior then prepares an independent appraisal. In others, the manager appraises his people and discusses the appraisal with each one. In still others, one or more people confer with the manager in preparing the appraisal. We will deal here only with the principles which the manager must understand in order to be an effective appraiser.

Regardless of the method employed, the manager is the key to the appraisal process. Hence it is most important that he be properly prepared. Preparation for formal appraisal begins with setting up a file folder for each subordinate. Throughout the year the manager records in the folder all pertinent information on the subordinate's achievements and failings, progress and conduct, contacts and reviews with him, and comments by others about him. In short, the manager should keep a comprehensive documented record of the subordinate. This is important because the manager must never criticize his subordinates without factual data to back him up. If a critical comment cannot be substantiated with fact, it is better left unsaid.

APPRAISAL TECHNIQUES. The manager should not appraise people he does not know reasonably well, particularly those who have recently come under his jurisdiction. He must have a number of contacts with a subordinate before he can appraise his performance.

Figures and data are always used for measurement. They are specific and on target as far as they go. But there are other, less tangible criteria that are equally important. For instance:

○ Is the subordinate willing to learn? He must be receptive to instruction, anxious to improve himself. When this quality is lacking, the manager is wasting his time.

- Is the subordinate trying to apply what is being taught? He may be a slow but thorough learner. It is the effort that counts. If the subordinate is not trying to apply what he learns, the manager is wasting his time.
- Does the subordinate's performance reflect steady improvement?
- Is he willing and able to handle problems on his own?
- Does he have the ability to apply instructions and training?
- Has he made progress in achieving his objectives?
- How strong is his drive, his motivation, his personal integrity? How about the pace at which he operates?
- Is he orderly and well organized? Does he use his time efficiently?
- Is he well regarded, well liked—a "nice person"?
- Does he have intellectual curiosity? Is he interested in things around him?

When an appraisal program fails to achieve its objective, it is usually because the manager:

- Appraises people he hardly knows.
- Is in such a hurry that he is careless.
- Is unconsciously biased in favor of or against a person.
- Employs incorrect standards of evaluation.
- Gives undue weight to recent events. (Remembers what happened yesterday but not what happened two, three or more months ago.)
- Wants all his people to "look good" when his superior reviews the appraisals.
- Uses flattering appraisals to win the favor of subordinates.
- Is afraid to give an adverse appraisal because he will have to discuss it with the subordinate.

○ Uses the appraisal to justify some other action, such as giving or denying a raise.

Here are some suggestions for making sound formal appraisals. Start by planning well ahead. Take the time to do a thorough job—do not become rushed or distracted. Study all the material for each subordinate and base your assessments primarily on accomplishment toward objectives. Appraisal should be an evaluation of performance, not personality, except to the extent that personality affects results.

THE COUNSELING SESSION

After the appraisal has been made, the subordinate sits down with the manager in a counseling session to answer three very important questions: "How am I doing?" "What do I do next?" "How can I do it better?"

Let's take a look at counseling in its broadest sense. Essentially, it is a discussion of job performance. It grows out of the coaching and appraisal that have preceded it. It may involve commendation or constructive criticism or both. Its purpose is to acquaint the subordinate with his strengths and weaknesses and *to develop an agreed-upon plan for improving his performance.*

Counseling may occur in a variety of settings—in an office, in front of a machine, out in the field, over lunch at noon. The manager usually begins with some complimentary remark. A bit of encouragement is always in order if counseling is to be effective. The counseling session should be a two-way street. The manager should try to develop such a close relationship with his subordinates that they will advise him in advance of their desire for counseling and of the subject to be discussed. Yet it goes without saying that the manager will usually initiate such a session.

Several benefits are to be derived from a counseling session:

- Counseling ties together the various points of the appraisal (formal or informal) and gives direction to the entire effort.
- The subordinate knows exactly how he is doing. His strengths and weaknesses are emphasized.
- Plans for the improvement of the subordinate's performance are crystalized.
- A strong personal relationship between the manager and his subordinate develops. The subordinate is willing to talk about his performance and how it can be improved.
- The tensions and anxieties that exist when a subordinate does not know what his superior thinks of his performance are reduced or eliminated.

Despite these advantages, some managers are reluctant to counsel with a subordinate. They find it difficult to discuss performance face to face. Such managers fail to understand that appraisal is useless unless it is followed by counseling.

Here are some suggestions for making the session successful:

1. Agree on a time when both parties are free from pressure.

2. Select a place where there will be no interruptions—no telephone calls, no urgent messages, no "it'll just take a minute" sidetracks.

3. Give the subordinate advance notice of the purpose of the counseling session. If the appraisal was formal, he should know who made it, who has seen it, and how con-

clusions were arrived at. He should have an opportunity to outline what he wants from this session.

4. Remember that the purpose of the session is to review and discuss the subordinate's performance and to help him improve it. Thus, performance must be discussed first, with personal qualities mentioned only when they affect performance.

5. Concentrate on discovering opportunities for improvement rather than baring weaknesses. Begin by discussing results during the period covered by the appraisal and the methods used to produce those results. What does the subordinate think of his record? Praise his strengths. Point out his weaknesses. Jointly resolve that before the session concludes, you and he will devise a program for his further growth and development.

6. Stay with statistical data, about which there can be little disagreement. Ask questions rather than make final judgments. Never try to be a psychologist unless you have the skill through formal training. Job performance is the manager's province, and this is where you should concentrate your efforts.

7. The entire session should be positive. The subordinate should feel that he is moving in the right direction—that he has been doing pretty well but is capable of doing even better.

8. As each subject is discussed, come to an agreement on a course of action aimed at improved performance. Avoid any argument or dispute that might engender hostility. Isolate areas of agreement and reach an understanding on appropriate recommendations for forward movement. Let any point of disagreement rest for the time being, unless the matter is vital and affects the tenure or ultimate success of the subordinate. There are usually enough areas of agreement to provide for a sound program.

9. Be prepared to cite specific examples to substantiate your conclusions, especially when they are negative. You must have proof of your allegations.

10. If the subordinate convinces you that changes in the appraisal are in order, they should be made without delay. Be willing to listen and to consider his point of view.

11. Managers are often guilty of paternalism. They give too much advice and try to do the subordinate's thinking for him. Encourage the subordinate to think for himself. *Listen.* Ask him how he thinks a problem can be solved, how he feels a matter should be handled, how he feels an obstacle can be removed.

12. The session should lead to specific steps to be taken. The subordinate is committing himself to a course of action to improve performance.

13. Summarize the results of the counseling session at its conclusion. Make sure the subordinate leaves the session encouraged and optimistic, with the feeling that he has received neither promises nor threats. He must be convinced that his manager wants to help him in every way.

14. The agreed-upon action now becomes the working basis, the track, for the manager-subordinate relationship. It is the program for achieving the next step in the subordinate's development.

PERSONAL AFFAIRS

The manager must find his job challenging, exciting, and interesting. But it must not interfere with his personal life. It must not make a widow of his wife or orphans of his children. Conferences and meetings should be minimized so that the manager has time for his major commitments.

Reports and written forms should be kept to a minimum. His job should not require regular "homework."

The personal life of subordinates is not the concern of the manager. In plain fact, it is none of his business. There is an exception: when the personal affairs of the subordinate affect his performance or the reputation and integrity of the organization. It is the manager's responsibility to step into such a situation promptly. Every subordinate must understand that no organization can retain anyone, no matter how valuable, whose personal conduct is injurious to its business and reputation.

Even though the manager should not be involved in the personal life of a subordinate, he can demonstrate a genuine interest in the subordinate and his family. When an employee's spouse is happy with his work, home becomes a place where the employee finds understanding, encouragement, and support for his efforts. The manager often tries to foster such an environment. His relationship is friendly but never intimate. Nothing he says or does must cloud the fact that he is the manager and represents management.

PLAIN THINKING ABOUT MOTIVATION

Many social scientists have spent years studying motivation. Many books on the subject have been written. But most operating managers have difficulty applying what they read or hear about motivation. All of us should continue to strengthen our skills in this area. In the meantime, here is some plain thinking about motivation as it applies to the managerial function.

The manager wants subordinates who are highly motivated to grow and develop. He wants them to know that he is there to help, that his objectives as well as theirs depend on working together as a team. The manager cannot succeed unless they succeed. If the subordinate is unhappy with his work, dislikes the manager, or feels that the organization is exploiting him, he will not be motivated to develop his skills and improve his performance. So the manager must create an environment that breeds motivation in subordinates.

Start by getting acquainted with each subordinate and giving him a chance to get acquainted with you. Take the time to sit down with him. Learn how to help him find satisfaction, happiness, and a sense of achievement in his job. Give him adequate compensation too, but recognize that this alone will never achieve high motivation.

What else does the subordinate want? He wants a boss he can look up to—a person who has character, works hard himself, and is frank under all circumstances. He wants someone who champions the organization and yet is the subordinate's representative to management when he has a complaint. He wants a boss who helps him over obstacles, who is confident and composed, fair but firm. He wants and needs recognition, both in his work environment and in his home and community. He needs to feel confident that he is topnotch in his work, that he can be proud of his skill and of his performance on the job.

How do managers know when they are motivating subordinates?

- When the subordinate says *we*, not *you* or *I*, in discussing business matters.
- When the subordinate is in complete agreement on objectives and works toward achieving them in the knowledge that they are attainable.
- When the subordinate brings his problems to the man-

ager without fear of criticism and knows that the manager will listen to him.

What can you as a manager do to motivate subordinates? Show that you have complete confidence in the subordinate. Make sure the subordinate understands his job and has been well trained. Don't police him. Give him the space he needs to do his job. (If the subordinate needs policing, perhaps you need a new subordinate.)

Give the subordinate real responsibility. It is risky to be sure, but a good manager must be willing to take risks, to overcome his fears. You will be surprised how often the subordinate comes through when he is given responsibility. Congratulate the subordinate on achievements. Compliment him whenever possible. Nothing succeeds like success, and the employee who achieves once is motivated to try again.

See that he gets recognition in his community—through newspaper publicity or other honors—as well as in his work environment. Give him the feeling that he is on the management team. Ask his advice on matters in which he has some skill or competence. Make sure he clearly understands what is expected of him so that he feels secure in what he is doing.

It is the skill of the manager that makes a motivated subordinate. Just as those most highly motivated to play golf are the best golfers, so the most highly motivated subordinates are those who, with their manager's help, have become the best performers in their work. Here are some examples of how to motivate a subordinate:

- Invite him to a meeting to speak on some achievement in his work.
- Have one of his achievements listed in the local newspaper. In one instance, a newspaper told about the in-

stallation of air conditioning in city hall and gave credit to the employee who sold the job and assumed responsibility for the engineering. In another instance, an employee who did an outstanding job in the community was awarded recognition as the "most community-minded employee of the year."

○ Write a letter to each of the subordinate's customers telling them that he has won an outstanding-performance award.

○ Establish a special club in the organization for high achievers. Membership is indicated by a pin and by special recognition at organizational affairs and meetings.

○ Print the subordinate's picture, with an accompanying article, in the organization's house organ.

What if a subordinate does not respond to the manager's efforts? Before passing judgment, the manager should examine his relationship with the subordinate to make sure that the fault does not lie with him. If the manager is not responsible for the subordinate's failure to respond, then the subordinate either is not capable of development or does not care to develop. In each case, it is useless for the manager to try to motivate the subordinate. He should spend his time with those who show possibilities for growth.

DISCHARGING A SUBORDINATE

Discharging a subordinate is one of the most difficult and distasteful of management jobs. Millions of dollars are lost each year because managers hesitate to discharge people who are performing below par. They say to themselves, "I'll give George another month. Perhaps he'll do better."

Or, "I think I see some signs of improvement in Doris. I'll keep her on a little longer." This is folly. When all the measurements tell the manager that the subordinate is not reaching his objectives—and is not motivated to do anything about it or is unable to do the assigned job—it is poor management to keep that person in the organization. It dilutes the manager's effectiveness and costs the organization money—money that could be better spent on worthy employees. To postpone action is inexcusable.

There are many yardsticks for determining whether a subordinate is doing well. The first is his progress toward agreed-upon objectives. The second is how well he responds to the counseling and coaching given him. There must be some evidence of progress, some indication that the subordinate is trying. If these two criteria are not met, the subordinate should be discharged.

The underachiever is better off in another job—for his sake as well as the company's. The poor performer knows he is not doing well and is not happy about it. This unhappiness manifests itself in his work and in his home life. His talents may be useful in a different kind of work, and it is best that he be encouraged to seek employment where he can be successful and happier.

The manager should set attainable standards with newly employed subordinates so that their progress can be measured. The manager does not want to keep new people if it becomes apparent that they should not have been employed. The new person should be subjected to a series of measures, like hurdles in a race. He must successfully jump one hurdle after another to remain in the race.

The new employee is jumping hurdles from the first recruiting contact. Each hurdle—each new task to perform—is a test of his competence to continue in the job. This process continues until he has qualified as a permanent member of the staff. The "test period" is important, so that people are not kept in jobs for which they are not qualified. It is a method of correcting errors in the selection of people and can save thousands of dollars and much lost time and effort.

THE OLD TIMER

What can be done about an older subordinate whose performance is no longer up to par? This consideration may be a factor in appraisal.

A person should be kept in a job as long as he or she can perform all the requirements according to established standards. Age alone is not a criterion for taking a person off a job. However, when a person cannot perform the job satisfactorily because of physical or mental disabilities connected with age, the manager is faced with a problem. There is a dual responsibility: (1) to the organization, which has to maintain a high standard of performance, and (2) to the subordinate, who has served the organization loyally for many years and has made a valuable contribution.

In a one-to-one conference the manager and the older employee should discuss the problems that arise when age reduces productivity. The organization should recognize its debt to the faithful employee who has served the organization well for many years. The older person must recognize that the organization must continue to move forward and that it cannot permit productivity to decline in any sector of its operations. Figure 10 illustrates the principle and can be used in a discussion between a manager and an older employee. Neither the manager nor the older subordinate wants productivity to decline with age.

Figure 10. Age and productivity.

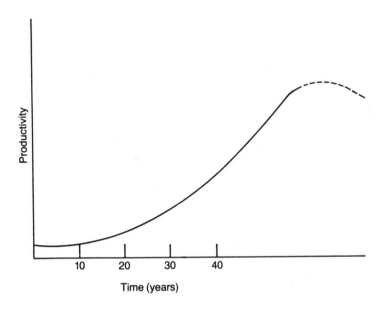

Time (years)

There are a number of alternatives to dismissal:

o The older person is assigned to other work. This may result in lowered compensation.
o The older person stays in his present job but is given an assistant. This sometimes, but not always, results in lowered compensation.
o The older person willingly gives up part of his job to another person. This often results in lowered compensation.
o The older person is given a special assignment. This may affect his compensation.
o The older person enters early retirement.

Generally, the manager should do all he can to keep the older subordinate employed in some way. It is debilitating for an employee to find himself with nothing to do after many years of active work. If there is no other alternative, the manager should try to find other work for the older subordinate through special agencies established for that purpose.

6

Control

Managers must be in control of the operations assigned to them. The manager is in control when (1) as a result of sound appraisal (formal and informal) and progress toward agreed-upon objectives, he knows how to improve performance, and (2) he applies this knowledge to improved planning.

Although the manager assigns part of his responsibilities to other people, he cannot relinquish accountability. Failure cannot be blamed on subordinates. The manager must be in control at all times.

THE PURPOSE OF CONTROL

Control is an important part of the Cycle of Management, discussed in Chapter 2. After setting objectives and developing a plan to achieve them (step 1), the manager and his subordinates start to carry out the plan (step 2).

Through review and appraisal (step 3), the manager periodically asks himself: "How is this operation going? What needs to be done to keep it running smoothly?" When he knows the answers to these questions and responds with positive action, he is in control of his job (step 4).

Controls are effective only when they transmit important information quickly. Controls fail when they are overly complex or detailed. They may be compared with traffic lights. It would be ridiculous to place copies of a city's traffic code at each intersection. A simple red light/green light system provides effective control.

To some people the word "control" denotes control over others. It is suggested here that control be thought of as a system that enables the manager to master those *tasks* that his superiors expect him to perform. The following items will inform the manager as to what he must control and what he must do to attain control:

- The job description. The manager must know how he is doing with respect to each responsibility listed.
- The agreed-upon objectives. The manager must know how he is doing with respect to objectives, which are more specific than the job description.
- The objectives of each of his subordinates. The manager must know when help is needed—when the signal is flashing "red."
- Statistical material. These important data tell the manager whether any new problems have arisen which must be handled promptly.

The manager is in control when he is doing something about each of his responsibilities, whether or not it has been delegated. He is in control when he sees and reacts to "red lights" promptly and effectively. One of the important benefits of controls is that they free the manager to devote his time to more important things. Most of us feel inundated by the mass of work we have to do. What should we do first? Some things are more important than others. Controls can tell us, or at least help us to decide, which matters urgently require attention and which can wait.

Good controls can even help us in allotting time for necessary tasks. In effect, a good system says: "You agreed to perform task **A** and now you must find the time to get that job done." Then it helps the manager find the appropriate time. A good control system will not let the manager forget anything. Of course, for the system to be of value, it must be examined carefully. The manager should set aside some time weekly for this purpose.

Too many controls may result in a manager *not* being on top of his job. He can become so preoccupied with the control function that he loses sight of his responsibilities. One field sales manager claimed he was so busy going over various controls in his office that he did not have time to go into the field with his sales representatives. Controls must be a help to good management, not a hindrance.

BASIC FINANCIAL CONTROL. The high-echelon manager must run a tight ship, with close control over operations. This means that he must catch incipient crises long before they erupt. He must seek out problem areas and make sure they are resolved. There are four special areas to be watched:

1. Profits. Compare with projection and with a year earlier.
2. Sales. Compare with projection and with a year earlier.
3. Accounts receivable. Is money coming in on time? If not, what can be done about it at once? This figure must never get out of hand.
4. Inventory. Compare with projection. Inventory levels

must not get out of hand. Make sure the figure does not exceed set limits. In a manufacturing operation, look at inventories of raw materials and finished products. Watch the percentage of full operating capacity measured against the projected percentage of capacity.

These keystones of control should be given high priority by management. Schedule the time to go over the figures thoroughly and carefully. If possible, have several members of top management do this together—the controller, sales manager (or vice president of marketing), and head of production (or operating head). Whenever a red light appears, dig into the reasons, find a solution, and report back. Do not let the matter slide. Do not rest until it is resolved. This is what is meant by *control*.

ORGANIZING THE CONTROL FUNCTION: A TIME FOR EVERYTHING

How is it possible to have a time for everything? By scheduling a time for everything! (Note: With a topnotch secretary or administrative assistant, there can be a time for everything. See below.)

In order to enjoy the feeling that comes from being on top of the job, it is important to set up certain control devices or tools. These will vary with each manager and his special needs, as well as with the nature of his responsibilities.

The manager has a considerable number of responsibilities, and he is expected to carry out all of them. This means that he must plan a specific piece of his time for each. How is this possible? Here is one way. (There are many other methods that work just as well.)

1. Prepare a control file—a list of all your responsibilities, whether or not they are delegated. This list describes your job.
2. Divide the list into two parts:
   ○ Responsibilities you elect to perform yourself. Make a file folder for each one.
   ○ Responsibilities you delegate to others. Make a file folder for *each person* to whom one or more of your responsibilities is delegated. On the inside of the folder list each responsibility delegated.
3. Determine, with your secretary or administrative assistant, what is to go into the folder. For example:
   ○ The strategy or plan for carrying out the responsibility.
   ○ Any figures, charts, data, or other material which is related to the responsibility and by which progress may be measured.
   ○ Any supporting material to aid in performing the responsibility (such as suggestions from superiors or co-workers).
   ○ Any observations that occur to you from time to time—any measurement that will keep you on top of the job.
   ○ A schedule showing how much time you have devoted to each responsibility and what to study before the next scheduled review.
4. When the file folder is for a person (someone reporting to the manager), it should also contain:
   ○ The agreed-upon objectives of the subordinate.
   ○ Statements and other figures indicating progress.
   ○ Notes, correspondence, and interoffice memos for discussion with the subordinate; any evaluations of him; any other matters for discussion at the next

review. All papers to be placed in file folders should be code-marked (such as PF for "personal file").

5. Schedule a specific time for reviewing each file folder.
    - Keep a diary (such as a "Week at a Glance") to govern the use of your time. Never assign the same time to more than one responsibility.
    - In the diary indicate a specific time on a specific day for reviewing each file folder. The time set for the review should have highest priority and should not be changed except in an emergency. If rescheduling is necessary, it should be done at once, so that *no file folder is ever without a scheduled time for review.*

6. Manage by exception. When red lights (problems, obstacles, retrogressions) appear during the review, bring out all the pertinent data for an in-depth study. Others who share the responsibility should be present. A plan of action should be developed at this time to correct the situation without delay.

Note that a key factor in the file folder system is that *everything about a single responsibility is in one place.* All the manager needs to know about the subject is at his fingertips. Additional material may be filed elsewhere for use when needed.

It is far better to concentrate on the material in a folder just before a scheduled review than to continually interrupt your work with a multitude of small matters. The former procedure utilizes your best thinking; the latter dilutes it. Another great advantage of file folders is that the many matters relating to a particular folder need not be handled the moment they come across your desk. They can be placed in the folder on receipt, to be handled when the subject comes up for review.

You should schedule uninterrupted time for office duties whenever possible. However, do set aside a block of time for phone calls, conferences, and unscheduled interviews so that you are accessible to those who wish to talk with you. Remember that you will remain on top of the job if you continually schedule a review of your responsibilities one at a time—whether you are performing the operation yourself or delegating it.

THE MANAGER'S OFFICE. Your office is your "control and communications center." Physical facilities vary widely, from a card table in a field sales manager's home to the lavish office of a top executive. But whatever the facility, it must measure up to these minimum requirements:

- It must be a facility to which and from which communications can flow.
- It must be a control center from which you can view your entire operation.
- It must be a center where tasks below your skill level are performed for you so that you can devote time to operating at highest skill—namely, the development of subordinates. (See Chapter 1.)

The manager should delegate to a subordinate (who is paid less than he is) all responsibilities that the subordinate can perform just as well or better, or can be trained to do. This is just plain good management. There is no economy in making a file clerk or stenographer out of a highly paid manager. The additional cost of an assistant will be amply repaid in the manager's improved and increased performance in the areas of his highest skills.

THE SECRETARY OR ADMINISTRATIVE ASSISTANT. The employment and training of a secretary or administrative assistant should have high priority. As you will see below, I am not talking about a private typist, file clerk, or a "gal/guy Friday" to bring in coffee and run errands. I am urging the employment of a mature, experienced assistant. Whether the manager needs a full-time or a part-time person is a matter to be determined individually. In any case, the manager must take responsibility for training the assistant as thoroughly as he would train any other subordinate.

A secretary or administrative assistant must:

- Know the manager's job from A to Z.
- Be tight-lipped—a *confidential* assistant.
- Be accurate.
- Prepare incoming mail so that all information needed by the manager is attached when mail is put on his desk. The manager can then act without delay. All incoming mail should be arranged in the order of its importance to the manager.
- Handle any dictating equipment or cassettes efficiently and accurately (see below). Cassettes completed by the manager while away from his desk should be promptly transcribed on his return.
- Keep the manager's calendar up to date.
- Prepare and give the manager all materials he will need for scheduled meetings and conferences.
- Keep the manager's folders and files up to date at all times. It is also the assistant's responsibility to place the file folder on the manager's desk on the day of the scheduled review of that folder.
- Understand the relative importance of the manager's phone calls and requests for interviews—without becoming a "wall" between the manager and others—and handle them with skill and understanding.
- Know what data and figures are needed by the man-

ager, know where to get them, and have them available
when needed. The assistant should be capable of scan-
ning these data and figures for important items and
marking them for the manager's attention.

o Recognize incipient crises and bring them to the manager's attention, with any supporting data available.

The kind of person I am suggesting may be compared with
the assistant to a radiologist. He or she receives the patient,
takes the X ray, develops the film, and turns it over to the
radiologist, who then employs his special skill to diagnose
what he sees on the negative and report to the patient or
his doctor.

DICTATING EQUIPMENT—HOW IT CAN HELP

Another tool of good management at any echelon is dictating equipment (including a portable dictating machine to
be used when the manager is away from his desk). Such
equipment enables the manager to take immediate action
on matters coming to his attention. Because dictation is
completed on the spot, it is more accurate than note taking.
More important, the manager need only consider the matter once. Otherwise, he has to make some notes and later
scan his notes, take time to recall all that occurred, and
dictate to a secretary. The secretary or stenographer also
has to do the job twice: once when she takes the dictation
and again when she transcribes it. The dictating equipment is handled only once.

"Never handle a matter or a piece of paper twice" is an
important rule. Here is how dictating equipment can help.

As a manager goes through his mail or concludes a
telephone conversation or conference, he can immediately
dictate the essence of what was said. The record, once

made, is complete. Pressure and tension are relieved. With the first reading of each piece of mail, he can dictate whatever action is required. In reviewing statistics, he can immediately—while bending over the figures—dictate memos, suggested action, directives, or notes to himself so that he does not need to go over the material again. He can dictate (1) replies to letters, with copies for files or for other concerned people; (2) confirmations of understandings, with copies to all concerned; (3) confirmations of telephone decisions, to insure complete understanding; (4) memos to the secretary or other people, with copies for file folders so that follow-up will materialize at the proper time; and (5) arrangements for meetings, setting time and place, with agenda and copies to all concerned and to file folders.

Some tips to save time when dictating: All materials needed for dictating should be on hand before you start. Then you need not stop to ask your secretary, who must also stop work to bring you additional materials. At the start of a piece of dictation, indicate the kind of paper, the layout of the dictation you require, the number of copies and to whom they will be sent, and all other information. In this way the dictation need not be typed over a second time. A folder should accompany each cassette. The typist can refer to the folder for spelling of names, addresses, and so on, thus further saving time.

Allot time for dictation. You can do three or four times as much dictation uninterrupted as you can when you are continually interrupted. For example, if the allotted dictation time is from ten to eleven on a given morning, have your secretary pick up all incoming calls and say: "Mr. Jones will be in at eleven o'clock. If you will leave your number, I will have him call you. I am his secretary. Is there anything I can do for you?" Then, at eleven, you can answer the calls. Those who wish to see you in person can make an appointment through your secretary for a time blocked out for that purpose. The same holds true when you are studying file folders, reviewing responsibilities, going over controls, studying statistics, or doing any other work that should not be interrupted.

On the subject of saving time, I should add as an aside that some incoming mail can be handled by writing a short memo on it, especially when no record is required. A reply to a subordinate may be a simple "O.K. Tom" written on the incoming letter and returned with date and the manager's initials. If a notation is needed, it can be made at once in the manager's diary.

INTERRUPTIONS

Interruptions are the principal cause for "I don't have the time." *Seldom is a matter of such a crisis nature that it justifies the interruption of a manager at work.*

Interruptions are usually caused by someone getting in touch with the manager at the other person's convenience—when the other person has the time and the inclination. The manager who is being interrupted is forced to delay other planned work, thus putting himself under pressure. If the manager is to be the master of his own time, he must decide how to use his time. If he allows others to make this decision, he has no right to claim that he does not have the time to do his job. He has in effect given away his time by allowing others to use part of it.

The most common interruptions are:

- Phone calls.
- People coming into the office ("It'll only take a minute").
- Stopping to read memos dropped on your desk.
- Unscheduled meetings (usually by superiors).

Here are some suggestions for avoiding interruptions. The secretary should screen phone calls when the manager is busy. The calls should be returned when the manager has scheduled time for them. (Usually the return call is no more than an hour or two later.) Those who wish to see the manager should make an appointment through the secretary. This can usually be accomplished on the same day but at a time convenient to the manager, not when he is busy with other work. The secretary should not interrupt the manager except for extremely important matters.

Conferences involving the manager should not be interrupted. This delays and prolongs them. Unscheduled meetings should be avoided whenever possible. Talk with superiors if necessary, since they usually do not wish to place roadblocks in the path of the manager.

Finally, subordinates should not make so many reports that the manager's time is taken up looking at them when more important things are left undone.

CONSCIENTIOUS MANAGEMENT

The manager should not go over the heads of his subordinates. The conscientious manager may do harm when, with the best of intentions, he steps into the shoes of a subordinate to solve a problem rather than *helping* the subordinate solve the problem himself. This can be one of the reasons why the manager "doesn't have the time" to do his own job. It is the manager's job to help his subordinates, but not to do their job for them. To do so wastes time and money, because the manager is performing a job that somebody else has been employed to do. It also breaks down morale and makes it difficult for subordinates to command respect and get results from others. ("Why should I go to my boss with a problem when I can go over his head to *his* boss and get attention?'') The manager's job is big enough to take up all his time.

When a crisis occurs, you should immediately reschedule all tasks that cannot be performed on schedule because of the crisis. Then call together key people involved in the crisis to develop an immediate course of action. Formulate new plans to replace the old plan. Implement the new plans quickly to get the operation back on track and moving forward. Finally, have your key people develop a permanent plan to take the place of the one that produced the crisis so it will not recur. Start to implement the plan right away.

A good manager must never panic. He must keep in control of himself and of his job.

Here is another idea for controlling responsibilities. After making a list of all your responsibilities, list on a ruled sheet all tasks to be performed *monthly or more frequently*. (See Figure 11.) Place an X under the day or days of the month when each task is to be performed. At the same time, enter the task under the same date in your diary. (Your secretary can do this monthly and place it on your desk on the first of each month.)

Next, on a second ruled sheet list all tasks to be performed *less often than monthly*. (See Figure 12.) Place an X under the month when each task is to be done. This sheet need be prepared only once a year. Enter each task in the diary on a day under the appropriate month.

Once a month the secretary will prepare a new sheet listing all tasks to be performed during the ensuing month, including a posting of all items from Figure 12 that have Xs under the current month. The manager will then have a complete list of all responsibilities to be handled during the current month and a time assigned for each one of

Figure 11. Actions to be taken this month.

May 19——	1	2	3	4 S	5	6	7	8	9	10	11 S	12	13	14	15	16	17	18 S	19	20	21	22	23	24	25 S	26	27	28	29	30	31
Review controls		X														X															X
Review important accounts					X														X				X								
R&D conference									X			X														X					
Plan contacts with Smith, Jones, Murphy, Kane					X							X							X							X					
Recruitment study			X							X							X							X							
Advertising & PR conference												X							X							X					
Correspondence		X							X							X							X						X		
Purchasing & inventory conference		X							X							X							X						X		
Set up control for next month																							X			X					
Acquisitions		X														X														X	
Review branch operations					X							X							X							X					
Expense study		X													X															X	
Conference with president														X																	
Moffat Division — conference						X	X																								
Cramer Division — conference								X																							
Pack-Rite Division — conference													X	X																	
Lanier Motor Division — conference																				X	X										
Forbes Wire Division — conference																											X	X			
Solar Mfg. Co.	X																												X		
General Mfg. Co.	X														X															X	
Acme Mfg. Co.														X															X		X

82

Figure 12. Tasks to be performed less often than monthly.

19—	JAN.	FEB.	MAR.	APR.	MAY	JUNE	JULY	AUG.	SEPT.	OCT.	NOV.	DEC.
Annual budget											X	
Appraisals, evaluations					X							
Annual planning sessions											X	X
Quarterly progress review	X			X			X			X		
Growth study	X		X		X		X		X		X	
Division conferences		X		X	X			X			X	
Manpower requirements						X						X
Forecast												X
Report to board												X
Production and manufacturing conference		X						X				
Marketing conference			X						X			
Finance conference				X						X		

them. The manager usually consults with his secretary on times when he will be out of the city or involved in special assignments.

Each day the manager reviews the tasks scheduled for the following day, and his secretary places on his desk the file folders for each task. No task will ever be forgotten or neglected. The manager will be in control.

7

Communication

It has been said that the word "communicator" is synonymous with "manager." Without good communication there cannot be good management. At the top, the manager must have a continuous flow of reliable and dependable information. It is his responsibility to encourage it.

In middle management, it is the responsibility of the manager to keep lines open so that good communication flows downward as well as upward. The middle manager must make sure that policies and procedures, rules and regulations—the "game plan" as developed by top management—is getting through to lower echelons. At the same time, his communications upward must reflect such matters as what is happening within the operating unit; employee attitudes; acceptance or rejection of policies and procedures; and quality and quantity of product being produced and sold.

DIRECT COMMUNICATION

The best type of communication is direct communication. Instruction, criticism, and counseling are most effective when performed on a face-to-face basis. The telephone is a valuable communications device, to be sure, but it is primarily informational and is not nearly so effective for instruction, much less for criticism. A letter can be used to confirm an understanding, to commend a subordinate, to formalize instructions in writing, or to prepare a subordinate for some action to be taken.

Printed matter sent to subordinates should be carefully prepared. If the information is to be preserved, it should be in a manual, technical bulletin, or similar form so that it can be made a part of operating tools. Information that need not be preserved can be in "throwaway" form. When printed matter is sent down through an organization, it is wise to attach a slip explaining its purpose and how it is to be employed.

Organizations spend a great deal of money making sure that information about their products or services gets through to prospective users. It may be worthwhile for such organizations to find out how to get through to their own people. Material should be concise and to the point, with graphs and diagrams whenever possible. Long paragraphs should be avoided.

Some managers feel that their superiors do not heed their reports and suggestions. If this is true and if the fault lies with the superiors, it is unfortunate. But more often, the reason is that the manager's method of communication is poor. The manager may transmit his views in a form that is difficult to grasp, inadequately prepared, or misleading in tone. In each case, their effectiveness will be diluted. The manager must realize that his superiors are just as busy as

Figure 13. Example of good upward communication.

Suggested Change in Policy Date: __________ From: __________	
Present Policy	
Advantages	Disadvantages
Suggested New Policy	
Advantages	Disadvantages
Summary	

he is and often equally frustrated. They want to have material submitted to them in a clear, concise form so that they can make a prompt decision. It is preferable to submit recommendations in such a form that only a yes or no is required. Figure 13 illustrates one kind of form for recommendations.

People in top management, or even in middle management, resent being told that they are wrong or "do not know their business." Instead of saying to a superior: "Such-and-such a policy is stupid," it is better to say: "I have studied the policy and noted certain problems. Here are some suggested changes for your consideration." Several copies of the suggestions may be submitted so that the superior can use them to ask others for their judgments.

An important duty of a manager is to report on his progress toward objectives. Since his job is, in reality, a piece of his superior's job, he should expect the same kind of help from his immediate superior that he gives to his subordinates. Good communication enables the manager's superior to assist him when needed. Ideally, the manager and his superior are in continual communication with each other, operating as a team.

Despite the obvious advantages of an unrestricted flow of information, barriers to upward communications sometimes develop. For example:

- To protect a manager he likes, a subordinate may keep bad news or uncomplimentary reports from him.
- If the manager is "throwing his weight around," the subordinate may be afraid to press his dissatisfactions.
- If the manager has failed to take action on undesirable conditions previously reported to him, the subordinate may feel that further reports would be useless.
- If the manager doesn't listen or dismisses the subject, the subordinate may stop communicating.

When the manager is negligent about communications, he may be jolted by the sudden resignation of a good employee. The manager must listen when subordinates talk. He must keep an open mind and be willing to consider suggested changes.

Communication is an integral part of the management function. It cannot be conducted in a vacuum, but must be viewed as one more tool for achieving objectives. It is closely related to interpersonal relationships and is vital to the manager's achievement and growth.

POLICY AND PROCEDURES MANUALS

Another important tool of good management is the manual. It crystalizes procedures in reference form so that a subordinate need not repeatedly go to his superior for information. In fact, it should be primarily a *reference manual*, a daily working tool for employees.

There is another important advantage to manuals: The manager need not spend an inordinate amount of time training and teaching a new employee. A good manual will do the job for him. In the manual the new subordinate can find exactly what to do, how to do it, and when it is to be done.

The first step in preparing a manual is to make an index or table of contents. Place the index in a looseleaf binder. Then have each subordinate write a detailed description of his operation. The subordinate should write up each new policy when it is put into effect, and each procedure as he performs the specific function, so that he does not have to set aside a large block of time for this purpose. The manual is prepared one piece at a time. As the sheets are written, they are inserted in the proper place in the binder. The accumulation of sheets becomes the manual.

The best manual is one that evolves over time. A manual will be obsolete soon after it is finished unless there is a procedure to keep it current—to delete policies and procedures that are no longer used and immediately insert new policies and procedures. Most organizations will have many manuals that provide written guidelines for all operations.

One person should be assigned full time or part time to keeping the manuals up to date. All manual changes then go to this person, who holds the master copies. The person in charge prepares the changes and sends them out with a simple note: "Please remove page No.— and insert the enclosed new page No.—." Manuals should be numbered, with a list of all those who have copies. Once every three to five years a completely new manual should be issued, since some employees will fail to keep their copies up to date.

COMPENSATION AND COMMUNICATION

Whole books have been written about compensation. The subject will be limited here to the relationship between compensation policy and a manager's responsibility to communicate both upward and downward.

Once a compensation plan has been decided upon, it is the manager's job to explain the plan to his subordinates, make sure that they accept it as fair and sound, and notify his superiors of any *general* dissatisfaction. He may also suggest improvements in the plan or its administration. To do this, the manager must understand certain principles of compensation administration.

Out of every dollar of income must come money for such things as raw materials, manufacturing, materials handling, research, office and administrative costs, selling expenses, taxes, and profits—as well as compensation of all employees. Each dollar must be divided among the various outlays, and no single item can demand more than its share—unless it can increase its contribution to the whole. This concept needs to be communicated down through the organization. If increased salary and wages can be offset by increased productivity, the balance between expenses can be maintained. But there must always be a balance. The manager must support the compensation plan, unless he feels it is inadequate and is prepared to bring his superiors a better plan.

Compensation is not a carrot. It should not be confused with various incentives employed to improve performance. Giving more money is not a substitute for good management. Compensation should, of course, include incentives for above-average overall performance, but not for specific tasks. The manager must be fully aware of the fringe benefits built into the compensation plan, which are often substantial. He should communicate their value to his subordinates.

Some determination must be made of how much an employee is worth and whether he is giving the organization its money's worth. By the same token, the employee must be helped toward a higher standard of living and must feel well compensated for the work performed. The vital question is not how much money an employee receives but how much he *earns*.

MEETINGS WITH SUBORDINATES

The manager often brings subordinates together for meetings, which can take one of three forms or a combination of them. These are illustrated schematically in Figure 14.

The first type of meeting is likely to fall short of its purpose. Those attending can be bored and tire of just listening. It is not conducive to good morale. It tends to put the listener in the position of an inferior and is authoritarian in nature.

The second type of meeting can be quite productive and is the most common form. The participants should be prepared and should have some contribution to make.

The third type of meeting requires more skill to chair but can be much more effective than either of the other two. Here full participation by everyone in the room often

Figure 14. Meeting patterns.

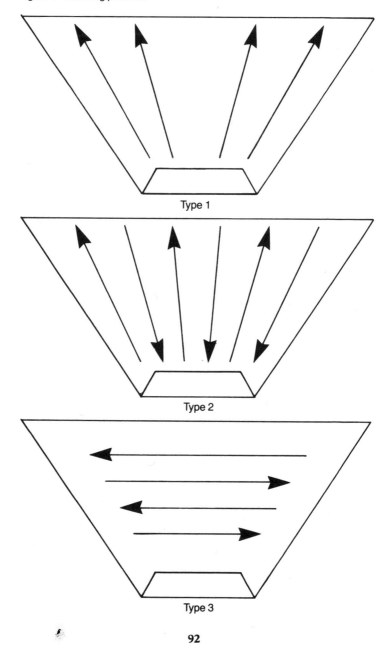

Type 1

Type 2

Type 3

brings new and better thinking. And since participation is so broad, acceptance of conclusions is also greater. The manager involves everyone but controls discussion, keeping the meeting on schedule and on the subject.

Here is an example of how the manager involves participants in the third type of meeting:

"For the next hour we will be discussing _____."

"Joe, you will recall I commended you on how you handled this matter when we got together on Smith Manufacturing. Will you tell the others what you did, what problems you ran into, and how you resolved them?"

"Thanks, Joe. Bill, what do you think of Joe's procedure?"

"Mary, do you have anything to add from your experience?"

"Mike, I know you've had experiences with this. How have you handled it?"

"Dave, you haven't said a word this morning. Let's have your thinking on this."

"Dave raises an interesting point. Joe, what do you have to say to his comments?"

"What would you do if _____ occurred? This has always been a problem. Mike, what do you think?"

Note that the manager involves everyone. He monitors and stimulates discussion; he summarizes but otherwise does not participate. Consensus is not important. What counts are discussion and thinking. When the hour has passed, close the discussion and go on to the next topic.

Meetings should not be called without good reason. When regular meetings are held at set times, the quality of discussion often deteriorates. The manager finds it hard to come up with things to talk about. Often, subordinates are bored and resent being called away from their work to attend a purposeless meeting.

Meetings should be set in advance so that subordinates have a chance to plan for them and to reschedule their work to fit in with the meeting. Let subordinates know the subjects to be discussed and suggest that they prepare for participation. The meeting should result in some action being taken, an action that is spelled out clearly and sent in memo form to those who attend. It may be placed in the file folder for discussion when the manager and his subordinate have their next review.

8

Recruitment, Selection, and Training

Managers with many different responsibilities will be reading this book. They will be employing people to fill every kind of job, from file clerk to top-level assistant to the manager himself. Each manager will need to adapt whatever of value appears on these pages. No effort has been made to cover the entire subject of recruitment and selection. Nor does everything written here have general application. With this in mind, the reader may find some methods or ideas to improve his operation.

RECRUITMENT

Managers often find themselves spending a considerable amount of time recruiting replacements. This takes them away from other important tasks. When an important person must be replaced because of death, illness, promotion, or discharge, the manager is pressed to drop everything and devote himself exclusively to filling the vacancy. If he fails to recruit under these circumstances, pleading pressure of other duties, he will be under tremendous pressure to fill one or more "slots" without delay. In the last analysis, the manager should personally select the people who will be on his team. He must take the time to make the choice.

The initial screening may be done in a variety of ways. The manager may find and employ his own people without any assistance. Or a personnel manager may screen and make the initial selections, from which the manager will make his choice. In large organizations an assistant to the top executive may be responsible for knowing the promotable people within the company. When a vacancy occurs, he recommends those people he knows to be most qualified.

Recruitment is a time-consuming task that must be done deliberately and thoroughly. The manager must discharge this obligation without pressure and without slighting other responsibilities. Another factor must be considered. The quality of the entire organization will depend largely on the development potential of the people employed. People recruited under pressure are not as likely to measure up to standards as are those recruited in a planned manner. If the manager is not careful in his recruitment and selection, he may find himself saddled with a mediocre person whom he must spend an inordinate amount of time with to develop. He is faced with trying to "make a silk purse out of a sow's ear." He will inevitably fail and have the entire job to do over again. In the meantime, his own performance will have suffered. He must find a way to do the job well, without expending too much time.

Whatever method is used for recruitment and selection, the new employee is "the baby" of his immediate superior, someone to train and develop. Ultimately, the quality of organization under any manager will be determined by the quality of people he is managing.

STANDARDS FOR RECRUITING. There must be some standards by which selection is determined. When a manager realizes his stake in an employee—in terms of workload, training time, and the sacrifice of other work—he will develop his own standards if the organization as a whole lacks them. These standards are of two kinds. First, the manager must have a list of all the duties the employee is expected to perform, with emphasis on the more important tasks. These are the *job specifications*. Second, the manager must ask himself: "What kind of person must I find to perform these duties? What type of qualities and background must the person possess?" The answers to these questions constitute *manpower specifications*. Do not start recruiting without both sets of specifications.

There are two additional tools that should be available for recruiting:

1. A personal history record or application form, to be in the hands of the manager before the first screening interview. It is a screening tool in itself, since it provides such information about the applicant as marital status, education, previous employment, and experiences pertinent to the applicant's qualifications for the job.
2. A fact sheet telling about the organization, its history, what it makes or does, who it deals with, the job to be filled and its requirements, the training to be given the new employee, and opportunities for growth.

Recruitment is a two-way street. It should provide a good person for the job and a good job for the person filling

97

it. Throughout the selection process, the manager should ask himself: "Is this a good move for the person I am interviewing?" Both employer and employee must feel they have made a good choice.

The cost of people is very high. Considering expenses—the costs of employing and training a new employee, supervisory costs, fringe benefits, and so on—it pays to recruit thoroughly and carefully. Managers often find it difficult to discharge an employee, and the cost of carrying an inadequate worker can be very high. On the other hand, an employee who becomes dissatisfied with his job is free to leave. In either case, the organization is the loser. The manager should take every precaution to find someone who has a better-than-average chance of succeeding and who feels that the job is an ideal opportunity.

THE POOL: A PRESSURE-RELIEVING DEVICE FOR FILLING JOB OPENINGS. Regardless of how applicants are found for a job, the fact that a slot is vacant is traumatic. The manager wants to fill the slot as soon as he can. Every job must be important; otherwise it would not exist. A job vacancy has a serious effect on the attainment of objectives, on the control of the operation, and on the efficient use of the manager's time. To avoid this, each manager should build a "pool" or reserve of eligible applicants for various jobs within his area of responsibility.

In developing the pool, the manager becomes a prime recruiter. He is continually looking for people who may be eligible for one of his jobs. Wherever he goes—at his club, in church functions, on business trips, in airplanes—he is constantly alert for good people. When others ask him about his business, he enthusiastically describes his organization and what it does, "selling" it to his listeners.

At all times the manager carries with him an application form and a description of the organization. When a listener shows interest, he leaves the form with that person, saying: "If you are ever interested in joining an organization like ours, send me this form and I'll arrange an appointment with you." The people he talks with are usually employed, but he takes their name, address, and telephone number and puts the information into a file folder called "pool," which is reviewed regularly. Top subordinates can help by performing the same function for the manager.

If the manager depends on a personnel manager or other sources for recruits, he will ask them to be alert for people who may be qualified to fill a vacancy. It is best *not* to wait for a vacancy to occur but to prepare for the eventuality beforehand. When good people are uncovered, an interview should be arranged—even if an opening does not exist. In many instances, neither the manager nor the applicant is ready to move, but the ground has been prepared for the time when the manager wants to act quickly.

Eventually, the pool folder will contain a list of a dozen or so people who looked good in a cursory interview and expressed some interest in a job opening "someday." When an opening occurs—and it often occurs suddenly and with little notice—the manager goes to his pool folder and gets in touch with one person after another, setting up interviews with those who are interested. Of course, a number of the people on the list will not be interested, but there will almost always be some who are. In this way, the job opening can be filled with a minimum of tension and pressure and without serious dislocation to meet a sudden crisis.

OTHER SOURCES OF RECRUITS. A few words to those managers who do their own recruiting. A top source for good recruits is present personnel. After all, they know the job, since they are in it themselves. When properly motivated, they can help the manager find good people. In some organizations they are rewarded for bringing in a new person.

People in other departments of the organization may welcome an opportunity to do the kind of work required in a manager's area of responsibility. The manager should use every possible channel to encourage applications for employment in his area from those presently employed within the organization. When employment in this manner is a promotion, the action should be encouraged. Promotion from within strengthens the organization by building high morale and making people feel that they can reach their goals within the present structure.

Employment agencies are often used to recruit staff. Be aware of the cost of this service. If you use it, limit yourself to one or two agencies at a time so that each will recognize that it has a special position and will work harder on your behalf. Contact the agency in person and talk with its head before contacting other individuals. It is important that the agency people feel they are filling an unusual opportunity. Sell them on the opportunity. Let them know that unless they can save you time and help you perform your job more efficiently, you will change agencies—you will only have two agencies at a time, but they must perform for you. Leave your personal history record or application form with them and give them a supply of fact sheets describing your organization and its opportunities for personnel.

Newspaper ads are another recruitment source. The main problem is that they are time-consuming. They bring in a large number of respondents, most of whom are not eligible for the position. It is best to use a box number for replies so that a filtering-out process can begin immediately. Those applicants who survive the first elimination can be contacted by telephone for further sorting out. The remainder can be asked to send in a profile of themselves, and an appointment can be set up to see them. Newspaper advertisements are usually run several times over two or three weeks before the filtering-out process begins.

Trade-publication ads have also been used for recruitment, with some success. Here again, the advertisement should be run over a period of time for best results.

Never rush recruitment. Take the time to do it right and do it thoroughly. A little care at this step may save many dollars and wasted time later on.

SELECTION

Different managers employ different people. The procedure for employing a machine operator in an office may not be as complex as that for employing someone who will himself manage a number of people or someone whose compensation will be high in the organization's salary structure. In general, however, the selection process should be thorough. It is far better to be careful in selection and have an employee who performs well than to rush the process and end up having to do it all over again. Let each manager keep this in mind as he reads these pages.

As noted earlier, the manager should be the determining factor in the employment of someone who is to help him reach his objectives. Therefore, whether he finds the applicant himself or uses the personnel department or other sources, he should play a key role in the selection process. Selection begins with the interview of the candidate. This interview should conform pretty much to the pattern outlined below.

THE SCREENING INTERVIEW. Managers often find selection interviews time-consuming and highly disruptive to their schedule. Here is one way to conserve time without diminishing the quality of the interview.

The first interview should be a "screening" interview. Its purpose is to eliminate applicants who do not qualify for one reason or another, and to lay the foundation for subsequent interviews with more promising candidates. How should this first interview be planned and executed?

The telephone interview is often the first step. Even if it is not a long-distance call, it should be carefully planned. The manager should be in control of the call and be prepared with questions. Answers to these questions will determine whether a personal interview should be scheduled at a fixed time and place.

Here are some examples of the kinds of questions to use in a telephone screening interview:

"Your name?"

"Are you presently employed? Doing what?"

"Have you ever performed ___(describe job)___ ?"

"For how long?"

"How many jobs have you had in the last ten years?"

A preliminary screening may also be made by having the applicant fill out and mail a personal history record, which will become the basis for determining whether to set up a personal interview.

THE PERSONAL INTERVIEW. The personal interview may be the only interview or it may be the first in a series, depending on the importance of the job being filled. In either instance, it is a critical step in the selection process.

The personal interview is a two-way affair. The manager wishes to learn whether the applicant meets the manpower specifications for the job. The applicant wishes to learn how well the job meets his requirements for security, opportunity for growth, and job satisfaction. Both parties are interviewing, so the process should not be one-sided. Nevertheless, the manager should be in control, guiding and directing the interview from the very start.

Some preparation will be expected of both individuals. The manager will have before him the applicant's personal history record or application form. The applicant should have received and studied the fact sheet about the organization and the job. (The applicant submits the application form when he requests the interview and the manager sends the fact sheet when he confirms the interview appointment.) Personal interviews may be scheduled late in the afternoon to conserve the manager's time and enable him to talk with the applicant when he is not under pressure.

Although each manager will conduct the interview in his own way, certain guidelines should be followed. Let the applicant do most of the talking. Do not be in a hurry to tell all about the organization and the job opening. The right kind of applicant will find out about the organization by asking questions. The important thing is to listen. Put the applicant at his ease so that he wants to talk. Suggest a procedure like this: "First tell me what you think I should know about you. Then you can ask me questions about the organization and the job, and I'll try to answer them."

Regardless of the kind of job, there are four basic qualifications to look for in any applicant: honesty, reliability, capacity for hard work, and pride in his work and his skill. In addition, the manager should determine certain personal traits of the subordinate. Is he down to earth and realistic, with good common sense? Does he describe himself thoroughly? Is he concerned with details, or does he gloss over his own life history? If he does, he may lack thoroughness in his work.

Does the applicant have a work history? Does he know what work is? Does he come from a thrifty home? Did he work as a youngster? Does he plan well? Does he have questions at the interview? Did he develop these questions beforehand? The applicant should ask questions that show his maturity (questions about training, opportunities for advancement when deserved, and the like).

If the manager reacts unfavorably to the applicant, he can terminate the interview at once without going into a long story about the organization. If the manager is interested, he should try to sell the applicant on the organization and make an appointment for a second interview.

The second interview should be extremely thorough, boring in on the applicant and his qualifications for the job. No questions should be spared. Here are some suggestions.

With respect to his previous job:

○ How did you get it?
○ What was the nature of the work when you started?
○ What was the nature of the work when you left?
○ What did you like about the job?
○ What did you dislike about it?
○ Why did you leave?

With respect to education:

○ Did you graduate from high school? From college? If not, why not?
○ What activities do you participate in?
○ What part of your expenses did you earn when you went to school?

With respect to family:

○ Tell me a little about your family—as much as you'd like to tell.
○ How did you spend Saturdays and leisure time after school?
○ At what age did you begin earning money? How?

With respect to the applicant's present situation:

○ Is your spouse employed? Doing what?
○ What do you do for recreation?
○ If married, how many children do you have?

Appraise the kinds of questions the applicant asks, the kind of planning he did for the interview, the thoroughness with which he tells about himself, the way he fights for the job. Does the interview increase your interest in him? Are there any gaps in his story that you want to dig into?

TESTS. In some instances, tests can be the sole basis for selecting nonmanagement personnel (service workers, machine operators or helpers, maintenance people, bus or train operators, and so forth). This is controversial at best but bears checking into.

For the most part tests can help in the selection process, but they are not a substitute for sound judgment. They are more reliable as a tool for eliminating unsuitable applicants than for selecting applicants. In the managerial echelons especially, there must be much more than just tests to determine an applicant's fitness for a job.

MULTIPLE INTERVIEWS. Ordinarily two or three interviews are conducted for candidates for high-compensation and managerial positions. The second and third interviews often reveal a different person from the first interview. The final interview, when the applicant is employed, should cover all the unfavorable aspects of the job as well as the favorable—to make sure the employee doesn't leave after six months because the job "isn't what he thought it was going to be."

INTERVIEWING SPOUSES. There are differences of opinion on whether an applicant's spouse should be interviewed. There is little disagreement, however, when the position will affect the spouse—for example, when it requires the applicant to be out of town a good part of the time, when it requires late or unusual hours, or when it entails a transfer from one city to another. There may also be a problem when an employee must work closely or even travel with an employee of the opposite sex.

The rule is that the applicant's spouse should be involved when the requirements of the position may cause dissatisfaction. Otherwise a good person may end up separating himself from the organization.

REFERENCES. Reference checks should precede the hiring of any employee. Although present laws are restrictive, some check must be made with previous employers. The investigation should be made in person or by telephone (even long distance), never by letter. Try to read between the lines, since employers will often drop inferences that give you important information.

When seeking references, talk to the person who supervised the applicant, not a personnel manager, who talks from a file rather than from experience. Imply that the job is important and pledge confidentiality. Consider such questions as these:

"Did he work under you?"

"He is applying for _____. How do you think he will fit into that kind of work?"

"Was he a hard worker?"

"How well did he get along with his boss? With his fellow workers?"

"Did he require more than average supervision?"

"Did he accept supervision?"

"Did he learn quickly?"

"Why did he leave your company? Would you rehire him?"

"About how much did he earn?"

"Did he have any personal problems?'

"What were his strongest qualities? His weakest?"

TRAINING NEW PEOPLE

Many good people are lost because of inept handling during their first few weeks of employment. The new employee should be treated as an important person. Training schedules should be kept. New workers should not be kept waiting for their superiors, nor should there be long delays in getting them into their jobs.

Generally, people learn best by doing, and teachers are at their best when they can observe others at work, correct them, and encourage them. A good procedure involves placing the new person at his job, explaining it to him, and having him repeat what he was told. The instructor then performs the job, explaining each step as he goes along. The trainee attempts to perform the job, is encouraged when he does some step well, and is corrected when he makes a mistake. The process is repeated until the employee can go through the operation without error. The procedure may take only a few hours in some work situa-

Figure 15. Learning patterns.

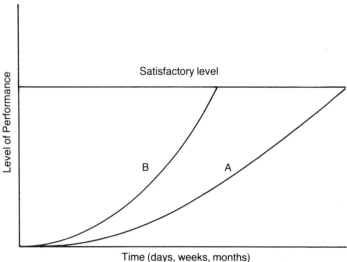

tions and two or three years in others. But the basic method is the same.

Modern equipment (such as audiovisual aids) can also be valuable training tools. New methods should continually be explored. Keep in mind that an effective training technique *accelerates* the development of the learner.

The learning pattern is portrayed in Figure 15. At one time the manager could be satisfied with the gradual growth of a new person (curve A). But today, with high compensation costs and the modern organization's need to move forward rapidly,the manager must be able to accelerate the development of a newly employed person (curve B).

The new employee must be evaluated continually during the training process. Three areas should be watched carefully:

○ How well does he *plan* his work assignment during training?

○ How well does he *apply* what has been taught?

○ How well does he *retain* what has been taught? Is he at ease in performing what he has learned?

Those who do not rate well in these three areas are questionable.

At the end of each training session, the manager and the employee should agree on the areas where progress is being made and the areas where more work is required. Weaknesses should be covered in subsequent training sessions, and the employee must make a special effort to master these areas.

How hard the employee tries to overcome his weaknesses is an important measure of his ability to "make the grade"—to continue in the job. The vital question is: Is he really trying? If he is not, he should be discharged without delay.

Every employee must be able to learn and apply what he learns. The manager must be able to accelerate the development of the new employee so that the job can be filled in the shortest possible time and the entire program moved forward.

9

The Manager's Role

THE MANAGER AS INNOVATOR

A good manager is eternally dissatisfied. He is always looking for a better way to perform. The effective manager continually asks: "Am I doing this job in the best way, or is there a better way to do it?" Here are some guidelines for being an innovative manager.

Develop an advisory team. Don't be a lone wolf. The final decision is still yours, but you can supplement your thinking with that of others in whom you have confidence. Your advisory team should be composed primarily of your own people. Others who may be called in by higher echelons of management are accountants, attorneys, bankers, and special consultants.

Go out among your subordinates—where your job is being done—and observe. Without going over the heads of subordinates, talk with people and get some of their thinking. Keep an open mind. Listen. Encourage your subordinates to bring ideas to you. Better yet, encourage them to test new ideas within their area of responsibility. This not only brings fresh thinking to the surface but also builds morale and improves performance.

Keep in touch with new developments by reading trade publications, going to seminars and trade shows, and listening to people who represent progressive corporations.

Try out new ideas. Do this on a small scale so that little is lost if an idea does not work. By trying out a variety of ideas you may find the one that will move the operation along. Keep a number of balls in the air continually—keep testing. Never say an idea is not good until it has been tried.

Top management needs to be alert to new ideas that will add to existing operations. Look for profitable operations that will fit into the work presently being performed and that will give you valuable manpower.

It is far better for your organization to be a leader in its field than to be a follower. The leader is more profitable, has manpower that is more alert and committed, and is accepted by potential customers as a front runner in the field. The follower is on the defensive, running as though in panic to catch up to the leader, often cutting profits to make up for being behind. Leaders are innovative.

THE MANAGER AS A PERSON OF ACTION

The manager must take action quickly when action is indicated. He cannot afford to be a procrastinator. We have been talking about good management and how to control operations so that the manager, through the review process, knows when action is called for. Strength in management will not brook delay. Here are a few spots where fast action, when indicated, is critical.

Operations that are unprofitable and inefficient should be discontinued. Why keep a losing operation going? Too often the manager is guilty of trying to justify continuing an unprofitable operation because it is painful to take action to discontinue it.

When new ideas have been tested and proved, they should be fed into the stream of operations at once. Every operation is always under pressure to be improved. When a better way is found, the manager must take action to put it to work.

When a new procedure is being tested and all indications are that it will not be useful, it should be discontinued promptly. It is often hard to give up a pet idea, but once it has had a fair trial and specific objectives have not been reached, it should be abandoned.

Reward top performers. Never let them become dissatisfied. When a person deserves recognition, make sure he gets it promptly. New employees who show exceptional aptitude and deserve promotion ahead of older employees should be promoted promptly. Good employees are often lost because management is too slow to take action when it is indicated.

Discharge poor performers promptly after they have been given a fair chance to improve their performance. A good manager must have measures for determining whether an employee is pulling his share of the load. When it is apparent that he is not, there is no excuse for keeping him. It is poor management and wasteful of resources to retain those who do not contribute to growth according to accepted objectives. Millions of dollars are wasted every year by managers who are too slow to discharge unprofitable personnel. Action should be swift when indicated.

The good manager is continually reviewing, appraising, and evaluating his operations and his personnel. This review process brings problems to the surface, where they can be resolved without delay. The good manager acts quickly to correct an adverse situation. By catching problems when they are small, he avoids big problems. After all, the manager is basically a problem solver.

One more thing: To act is to take risks. The manager who is afraid of the risks involved in taking action is not a good manager. Good management is not for timid souls.

The watchwords of good management may very well be REVIEW—REACT—ACT.

THE MANAGER AND THE COMMUNITY

There are at least two important reasons for the manager to be involved in the community. The first is his responsibility to his organization; the second, his responsibility as a good citizen. They are equally important.

The organization has a responsibility to create an image that gives it respect and confidence—in its goals and the methods it uses to attain them. This is particularly applicable to business organizations but also applies to hospitals, educational institutions, and all other kinds of organizations. The world of trade and commerce is not an evil giant preying on the little citizen. It has provided employment, financed research, and developed new and better methods for working and living. The manager must make certain that his organization deserves the confidence of the community in which it operates. He must defend his organization against unwarranted attack and seek to improve the organization where it is lacking. The manager wants to attract the best employees to his organization, and he wants to build support for the organization when community approval is sought for its projects.

The manager should be active in the community, but his activities should not encroach on the time required to perform his job. There are many ways to be a good manager and a good citizen at the same time.

The manager should be informed about the local, state, and federal goverment. He should be equipped to intelligently support or oppose vital issues. He can serve on library boards, school boards, or boards of philanthropic agencies—all of which provide no compensation except the satisfaction of being a good citizen. In performing such work the manager also enhances the image of his organization. And within the organization he must work to develop a sense of responsibility to the community.

SUMMING UP

Essentially, the manager's job involves selecting and developing capable people. Andrew Carnegie, founder of the Unites States Steel Corporation, reportedly said: "Take away all my steel mills. Take away all my money. Leave me my people and in five years I will have everything back."

To summarize all that has been said in this book:

o Know your own objectives.
o Get the right people to help you achieve them and train them well.
o Give each subordinate a specific piece of your total job and the responsibility for performing it.
o Set agreed-upon objectives *with* each subordinate so that each can continually appraise his own performance.

o Work closely with each subordinate to help him reach his objectives.

o Review, review, review. Keep asking: "How are we doing?" Counsel with your subordinates to obtain agreement on action to improve performance.

o Always know the next step to be taken to carry out each responsibility, and when it must be taken. In this way you will be in control of the total job.

o Motivate subordinates so that they *want* to do what you are asking them to do.

Index